TAKING BACK MY LIFE

Nancy Ziegenmeyer

WITH

Larkin Warren

SUMMIT BOOKS
New York • London • Toronto
Sydney • Tokyo • Singapore

SUMMIT BOOKS
Simon & Schuster Building
Rockefeller Center
1230 Avenue of the Americas
New York, New York 10020

Copyright © 1992 by Nancy Ziegenmeyer
All rights reserved
including the right of reproduction
in whole or in part in any form.
SUMMIT BOOKS *and colophon are*
trademarks of Simon & Schuster Inc.
Manufactured in the United States of America

10 9 8 7 6 5 4 3 2 1

Library of Congress Cataloging in Publication Data

Ziegenmeyer, Nancy.
   Taking back my life / Nancy Ziegenmeyer with
Larkin Warren.
      p.   cm.
      1. Ziegenmeyer, Nancy.   2. Rape victims—
Iowa—Biography.   I. Warren, Larkin.   II. Title.
HV6565.I8Z54   1992
364.1'532'092—dc20
[B]   91-38156
                                                   CIP
ISBN: 0-671-73455-5

"A Few Good Things Remain" by Jon Vezner and
Patrick Alger. Copyright © 1990 Sheddhouse Music,
administered by Polygram International Publishing,
Inc.
Editorial page © 1990, 1991 The Des Moines Reg-
ister and Tribune.

FOR STEVEN
AND THE CHILDREN,
WITH LOVE.

"When the world outside my window
goes insane,
you're here to remind me
A few good things remain."

PROLOGUE

THE DAY the people from the "Today" show tracked me down at the airport in Des Moines was the day I decided I was ready to curl up in a ball and quit. We were standing there, my lawyer and I, waiting for the plane that would take us to Chicago and then on to Washington, D.C., when suddenly we heard his name over the public address system. "Mr. Olson. Mr. William Olson. Please pick up the nearest courtesy phone." The words came through the air like the very pleasant but authoritative voice of doom. It made us both jump.

Bill went off to find out what was going on, and when he came back, he said, "It was the 'Today' show. They know where you are, they know where you're going, and they want you to be on tomorrow morning."

My hands started to shake, and whatever I'd had for breakfast that morning was threatening to come back up. It wasn't as though I was Madonna, or a stumping presidential candidate (something often seen here in Iowa). What was it that had brought me to this point? Why did a call from what was probably a perfectly nice person from NBC make me break into a cold sweat? And where could I go to hide?

As soon as I could, I ran and found a pay phone and called a friend. "This isn't what I meant . . . it isn't what I thought it would be," I blurted. "They can always find me now, no matter what I'm doing. I want it all to stop; I don't want to talk to any more reporters. No more details, no more personal stuff. It's just too hard now." I could hear the panic in my voice, and a fear that had become very familiar.

My friend listened patiently as I talked my way through my fit, and then we talked a little longer, reminding each other of all the things that had happened to lead me to this time and place in my life. When I'd finally calmed down a little, I said good-bye, hung up, and headed off to meet Bill at the departure gate. I was on my way to testify before a Senate subcommittee on behalf of a new crime bill, the first major federal legislation dealing specifically with violent crimes against women. I was going not because I was a lawyer, or a legislator, or a cop, but because I was a victim.

The crime was rape, some bastard's bad idea of a good time. After it happened, after the arrest, the trial, and the verdict, it had been my decision to tell the story, in my hope and belief that telling it could make a difference to the women and men who survive this crime and must somehow remake their lives in its aftermath.

But I never could have anticipated what would come next— the reporters, the cameras, the phone calls, the letters, and the constant threat that less and less of my life with my husband and children would remain my own. And one by one, as each detail of my story came out, every secret that I'd ever had was being told. Some were good secrets, harmless secrets. Some of them were not.

Through it all, I could hear my grandmother's voice, teaching me when I was a child about telling the truth. "Nancy Jo," she would say, "you're only as naughty as your secrets. And if you don't have any, why then, you're not naughty."

It took years for me to learn the lesson of truth versus secrets, and just as I've had to learn everything else, I learned it the hard way. Truth never meant more to me than it does today. There are other voices in this book who saw what happened, although maybe from perspectives different from my own. But they were all there. So here it all is, from me, from them—the truth.

CHAPTER ONE

THE DAY OUTSIDE looked like pea soup. It was barely
light out, a little after 5:00 A.M., and the fog was so
thick I couldn't see the street from my bedroom window. It was
hard to drag myself out of bed when the alarm went off—I'd
stayed up until midnight the night before, studying, trying to
cram in every last tiny bit of information. It reminded me of
high school.

Steven had already gotten up, and while I showered, he
went downstairs and made coffee. It was blessedly quiet—it
was way too early for the children to be up. We've never been
cheerfully chatty in the morning, like the couples in the in-
stant coffee ads on TV—there's usually too much going on
around us to do much more than eat, deal with the kids, and
run—but it was nice, this one morning, to be by ourselves for
a bit.

I'd been studying hard for the real estate test I was to take
later that morning in Des Moines. Passing it would mean an
Iowa real estate sales license. It would mean no more waitressing, no more bartending, no more leaning so heavily on
Steven for the money that a family of five needs to get by, even
in a small town like Grinnell. I was scared to death of the math
part of the test, and when I was learning to use the calculator,
my fingers seemed to be all over the place, pushing the wrong
buttons and coming up with the wrong answers. But I'd done
well in the prep course, driving back and forth to Des Moines

9

every day, sitting there for eight hours, forcing my brain to learn new things. I thought I had a better-than-even chance of passing. It would mean a change in our lives, a change we badly needed.

The fog meant leaving earlier than I'd planned. The test was at 7:30, and Des Moines is just about an hour away. But I wanted to get there in plenty of time to take a last, calm look at my notes. I quickly ran upstairs to wake the kids and kiss them each good-bye. Nicholas and Ben sleepily wished me good luck, Sissy just made a little face and rolled back over into her pillow. I said something about maybe all of us doing something special that night—it was Saturday, after all—but I knew that what I'd probably do was come back home and sit around and worry and wonder how I'd done on the test.

Steven threw a jacket on over his T-shirt and jeans and walked me out to the driveway, watching while I unlocked the car door. "I guess we'll see you sometime after lunch," he said. "Good luck. And be careful."

I tossed my long denim coat onto the backseat and slid into the driver's seat. After buckling the seat belt, I quickly checked my hair and makeup in the rearview mirror. You idiot, I thought, it's a little silly to worry about how you look and what you're wearing at this point. It's not like they'll notice the new red turtleneck sweater or give you extra points for a good haircut.

I waved good-bye to Steven, then backed out of the driveway, looking at the dashboard clock as I turned out of our street onto Sixth Avenue. Just 6:00 A.M., plenty of time.

When I got to the Kwik-Shop in Grinnell, I stopped and bought a Coke. Not the best nutrition at that hour, but I knew the sugar would give me the jump start I needed after only five hours of sleep. I lit a cigarette (I'm as stubbornly unreformed about smoking as I am about sugar), turned on the radio, which was tuned, as always, to 92.5, KJJY, the country station, and headed for Interstate 80.

The car, a dusty-blue GrandAm, was practically brand new, fun to drive, even more fun to drive fast. As I drove, I hummed along with the music, trying to ignore the test jitters. George Strait was singing "If You Ain't Lovin', You Ain't Livin'." I pictured Steven and the children back at the house, and the way their morning would go. The kids would probably stay in their pajamas for a while, watching cartoons on TV, getting bombarded with all the pre-Christmas advertising that had begun already despite the fact that it was only November 19, not even Thanksgiving yet.

I was really looking forward to the holidays. Steven and I had been through a terrible time in our marriage, but we'd battled it all out. There were still some sore spots, days when we tiptoed around each other as if we were living in an intensive-care unit. But it had finally begun to look as if we were going to make it. I would be twenty-eight in January, and was growing more and more excited about the changes in our lives. If I did well on this test today, it would almost be like icing on the cake—it could really change everything.

As I approached the edge of Des Moines, I lit another Virginia Slim, trying to push back my growing case of exam nerves. On the radio, Rosanne Cash was singing "Runaway Train." "I'm worried about you, I'm worried about me, Curves after midnight aren't easy to see," I sang along. The closer I got to the exam, the faster I drove. When I finally turned into the parking lot of Grand View College's Science Building, where the test would be held, I checked the dashboard clock: 7:05. Good, I had almost a half hour to review my notes.

I parked the car and cut the ignition, unsnapped the seat belt, and reached for my bookbag. My glasses and contacts were probably buried at the bottom of the bag, and I decided not to bother digging them out. Instead, I pulled out my notebook, opened it, and started to read.

Suddenly the driver's door opened and somebody reached in and grabbed my neck. "Move over!" a male voice demanded.

Startled, I looked up to see a young black man pushing his

way into the car. I instinctively raised my hand to push him away, to hit or scratch, and felt a sharp pain in my right hand when I caught him with a fingernail. I could smell alcohol on his breath, on his clothes. He was quicker and stronger than I, with the element of surprise on his side. With one hand he grabbed my arm in midair, with the other he covered my face with some kind of white cloth. I tried to twist away, to scream.

"Quit fighting," he said, "or I'll kill you." His voice was almost calm. Then he shoved me across the car, over the console, into the passenger's seat. He held me there, reaching over for the lever that dropped my seat into the recline position. He grabbed my coat from the backseat and roughly pulled it down over my head. Gasping for breath, my heart thudding in my chest, I remembered what the parking lot had looked like when I had pulled into it only minutes before: It had been empty.

"Where's your money?" he said.

"It's in here, right here." I gestured with my left hand at the console between the two seats.

"Get it out," he said.

Blindly, I fumbled around with the money in the console, three or four dollars in bills, probably another three or so in change, and handed it over in the direction of his voice, where I thought his hand might be.

"I don't want the change," he said, taking the bills. "Put it back in there." And then, "I'm not going to hurt you. Where's your purse?"

"It's in my bookbag, but there's no more money in it. Really, there's nothing in it. But you can look if you want." My voice sounded funny to me, underneath the coat. What a joke at that point, giving him permission to look in the bookbag.

"Get your wallet out of there," he said. The bag was on the floor in front of me. When I reached into it for my wallet, I looked down from beneath my tent. I could see that the fingernail on my right-hand ring finger was almost completely torn off, all the way down to the quick. It was bleeding, the nail just hanging there. I held the wallet out in his direction, showing him there was no money in it. He told me to put it back in the bag.

I heard a clicking noise and felt the slight "thump" as he adjusted the driver's seat back. Then I heard the car start up, and I knew I had to somehow get out. I leaned forward slightly, and started to slip my right hand out from under the coat toward the car door. I would have to unlock it and open it almost in the same motion. I always kept all the doors locked because of the children. Except my own door. When I'd gotten into the car that morning, I'd forgotten to lock my own door.

He must've seen the movement, must've thought I was trying to pull the coat off my head, because he shouted, "Don't look at me, or I'll kill you!" and slammed me back down hard against the seat. It was the only time he'd raised his voice. and it had the effect of a slap. I assumed he had a weapon. I had no way of knowing if he didn't.

When he started the car, KJJY came back on. He immediately punched the buttons until he hit a rock station. Then the car began to move. He changed the music, I thought. He changed my music. We picked up speed as he turned out of the parking lot. I won't be able to get out. Is he going to kill me? Where is he taking me? Why doesn't he just take the car and leave me alone? Then he started to talk, to ask me questions.

"What were you doing in that parking lot?"

I told him I was there for the test.

"Do you work?"

I told him no, not now.

"Then how did you pay for this new car?"

I told him my husband had paid for the GrandAm. He wanted to know where Steven worked, what he did, and I told him that, too. And I told him I had three children.

I might as well have been blind under the coat, helpless, terrified. I'd never see Steven again, never see my children. I was going to die. Once that thought came into my mind, it was followed by another: I knew I had to get a grip on the fear somehow. But how?

Suddenly I could hear Steven's voice inside my head, his low drawl, quiet and deliberate. Calm down, Nancy, it said. Pay attention to what's going on around you. Listen to his voice. Watch for details: clothes, jewelry, scars, birthmarks. Feel the car as it moves: What direction does it seem to be going? Left? Right? What can you hear?

I could hear the sound of gravel under the tires as we turned. Into a driveway? Then the man honked the horn twice. Was it a signal to somebody? I slowly, carefully peeked out from under the coat, to my right, and briefly saw a large, light-green house. Institutional green. Was I going to be taken into the house? Where there more men? Were they going to come out and get into the car?

We waited there a minute, maybe two, but I didn't hear anyone come out. He didn't say a word, then he started to back out. Just for a moment I felt relieved—no one was coming out, and we weren't going in.

As the car moved, I quickly looked again and saw a big front porch with steps going up to it. The porch looked like it was brick, and it had at least one pillar, maybe a corner pillar. And I could see a number on the pillar: 1320. I tried to look for a street sign so I could at least tell someone what street it was on, but I was too far back in the seat; I couldn't see the signs. And who would I tell if I saw one, I wondered, and when?

He drove around some more, turning and turning. He started to talk again. He talked about white people. He said his father had been shot by a white person, and there had been a trial. After the trial was over, his sister had been raped by a white man. Because she'd testified at the trial she was beaten and raped, he said, and that was what white people had always done to black people. What white men had always done to black women.

"But I'm not going to rape you," he said. "You don't look

like you're worth the trouble. And I'm not going to kill you, because you've got kids. I know what it's like to grow up without a parent. I grew up without a father."

He asked me if I'd voted in the presidential election. Scared to say the wrong thing, I lied and said no. It was the wrong answer, and he got agitated. Well, then, if I had voted, he wanted to know, who would I have voted for? Trying to figure out what the right answer would be for him, I lied again and said George Bush.

He said, "It figures, you white bitch."

He drove silently for a minute or two, then made a sound, almost like a "tsk, tsk." "You must smoke like a chimney, this ashtray is full of cigarette butts." I didn't say anything.

"Are you a real redhead?" he asked. All I could think of was that he'd said he wasn't going to kill me. Did he mean it?

And then he stopped the car again. I cautiously turned my head to the right, peeking out from under the coat. We were in a parking lot. Out of the corner of my eye, I could see part of a building. It had crooked eavespouts. And then he moved toward me.

He unzipped his pants. I could see his hands, and I heard the zipper. He grabbed his penis with one hand, and grabbed my head, pulling me across the console, with the other.

"Put it in your mouth. Make me come, you bitch. And if you bite me, I'll kill you."

I did as I was told and as I did, something went cold inside me. All I could see was a blue, shimmering light, like crystal glowing somewhere way in the back of my head. I wanted to reach out for something safe, but only the blue light was there. I couldn't even think of what was happening in terms of a sex act. All I could think of was death.

"Have you ever done this before?" he asked. The coat still over my head, I could feel myself hyperventilating and knew I had to stop, knew I had to keep from screaming, keep from gagging.

He suddenly grabbed me by the shoulders and pushed me

face down on the console, yanking at my tights and my underpants. My arms were bent funny underneath me. His full weight was on my back as he tried anal sex. It was as though someone had hit a switch, and my body had shut off. Only my mind was working, part of it insisting this isn't happening, this isn't happening, the other part oddly focused. It was clear he wasn't being successful. I was scared of the anger that might follow his failure.

He shoved me back over to the passenger seat, then reached down to the floor, picked up my bookbag, and threw it onto the backseat. As he moved toward me again, I clenched my hands together in my lap, trying to hold my jumper down.

"Move your hands," he ordered, pushing, then pulling at the fabric of my dress. "Move 'em!" I let them fall to my sides, the left one on the seat, the right one down between the seat and the car door.

"How does it feel?" he asked, moving above me. "Have you ever made love with a black man?" His body felt calm. He wasn't sweaty, his muscles didn't seem to be clenched, he wasn't even breathing hard.

I had shut my eyes so tight I could see stars behind my eyelids. Death was in the car, I knew it. I'd never see the children again. I thought of Sissy's ballet lessons, the boys, their piano lessons, the piano in my living room, and the children sitting at it. Would Steven make sure they practiced? Then I heard Steven, his voice inside my head again. Pay attention to what's going on around you. I opened my eyes.

But what could I see from under my tent? A blue suit, I thought, some kind of stripe running through it. Pinstripes. White shirt, or maybe pale blue. No tie. No scars or birthmarks from what I could tell. No jewelry on his hands. And white sweat socks. Odd, with a suit.

After he'd ejaculated, he got off me and moved back to the driver's seat, pulling up his pants.

"I hope you didn't give me AIDS, you white bitch," he said.

I wanted desperately to cover myself, and began to fumble on the floor for my underwear, my tights.

"Keep your head covered," he snapped. "Wait until we get going again." And the car once again began to move.

I struggled awkwardly to get dressed as he drove, five, six, seven minutes. I pulled up my underpants, white cotton ones, with little blue dinosaurs on them. That's funny, I thought. I pulled up my tights, and tried to smooth down my jumper. My hands were in fists. There were tears in my eyes, but I didn't make a sound. I won't cry, I thought. I won't cry. I won't give him that.

When he finally came to a stop, it seemed as if we were in the same parking lot we'd just left, the one with the building with the eavespouts. Oh, God, I thought, this is going to happen all over again.

"Are these real?" he asked, grabbing my left hand. "Yes," I mumbled, and felt him pull my wedding band and engagement ring off my finger.

"Is this real gold?" he asked, holding my wrist as he fingered my watch.

"No," I answered, "it's a Wally World special," then realized that our joke name for Grinnell's Wal-Mart probably wouldn't mean anything to him. He dropped my arm and left the watch where it was.

My head was still covered by the coat, so he didn't see the diamond studs in my ears that matched the engagement band, or the diamond chip on a chain around my neck, or the little sapphire ring on my right hand, on the finger that still bled.

Then he picked up the white cloth he'd first used to cover my face and carefully, almost gently, wiped off my fingers, my hands, my arms. Just as carefully, he began to wipe off everything in the car he might've touched.

"I should tie you up and throw you in the trunk," he said. "I should just tie you up and throw you in the river." He reached back and pulled my bookbag over to the front seat and started going through it. My real estate books, my notebook, purse, glasses, contacts. My address book. My driver's license, with my name and address on it.

"If you go to the cops, I'll come after you," he said. "I know where you live now, you and your kids. My brothers will come after you, and they'll get you. Go home to your husband. You're white, you'll be OK. You can get a counselor. And if you tell the cops anything, you better tell them you were raped by a white man."

Then he ordered me to get down on the car floor and stay there for at least ten minutes.

"I've got people out here, they're watching the car. They're going to follow you, make sure you get on the Interstate."

Did they follow us when he drove up to that house, when he signaled with the horn? I wondered.

He opened the door and got out, taking my bag with him. I heard the door slam.

Keeping my head down, I hurled myself across the seat and hit the car door button, locking myself in, then pulled the coat off my head, gulping air like it was water. After about a minute, I slowly got up and looked around. He wasn't out there. The parking lot was empty. I didn't recognize it. The clock on the dashboard read 7:35. I didn't know where I was. I was lost.

CHAPTER TWO

ALL I WANTED to do at that point was lie down on the car seat and sob. But I didn't know if anyone, his brothers, his watchers, were keeping an eye on me. I knew I had to get out of there, wherever "there" was.

I started the car and, with the tires screeching, I turned out onto the street, a side street of some kind, and drove around blindly, looking for some kind of landmark, a street sign, a building, an Interstate sign, a store, anything that would tell me where I was and how to get back home.

I was going around in what felt like circles, sure that I was being followed, sure that if I stopped to get my bearings the nightmare would start all over again. The only control I had was keeping my foot down on the accelerator and my hands clenched on the steering wheel.

Suddenly I recognized Mercy Hospital, the medical center where I'd taken the children for doctors' appointments. I yanked the wheel around hard, swinging into the parking lot. But I can't just leave the car anywhere, I thought numbly, they'll tow me. So I drove around and around until I found a free parking space.

When I got out, I locked the door behind me, thinking that's stupid, there's nothing left in it to take. I ran to the emergency room entrance, not looking for medical attention—I knew I wasn't hurt—but only wanting safety, to just get inside someplace, to get out of danger. My breathing was coming faster and faster, and I was sure now that I'd been followed, that he was running right behind me, that I could hear the slapping sound of his shoes on the pavement.

Once through the door, I began to fall apart. Now I was free to hyperventilate, to gag, to cry, to make noise. It felt like my arms and legs were going to fly off my body.

"I've been raped," I said loudly to a waiting room full of shocked, silent people. It seemed they were gaping at me. "Please, I've been raped!" I cried. A nurse appeared from somewhere and gently took my arm. At first I shook off her touch, the first physical contact I'd had since he, the rapist (for that's who he was to me now: The Rapist, My Rapist), had taken my rings from my finger. But the nurse was careful, and tried it again. I looked closely at her, at her white lab coat. Her name tag. Deborah Smith, it said. She was whispering something as she led me into another room, away from all those eyes.

She steered me to a chair. What was my name? I told her. Then I asked for a glass of water, a cigarette. No, Deborah said. Nothing to drink, nothing in your mouth. It'll destroy evidence. Another nurse had come into the room. Another person to decide to trust. Beverly Clark, her name tag said. I thought, how nice they're dressed in white, just like nurses are supposed to be. The white seemed like a nice, quiet color.

"We want to call the crisis center for you, Polk County Victim Services," Deborah said. "They will send a counselor to the hospital, to help you through the doctor's examination. Then she'll stay right here with you when the police come, to help you with the report."

The police? Wait a minute. No police.

"I've seen this on TV!" I cried. "They'll blame me. And Steven will blame me, and then they'll take away the children. It wasn't my fault! This time I've really done it; this time he won't be able to forgive me!" I put my head down on the table and wept. One of them put her hand on my shoulder, very gently.

I knew how it would go. The police never believed the victim, they'd look at her—no, me, they'd look at me—and snicker. Even if they went after him, even if they caught him, they'd get me into court and drag my whole life out for people to look at, every stupid thing I ever did, or wore, or said; everything that Steven and I had been through. And the mere thought of an examination, of someone touching me where that man had touched me . . . oh, God, I wanted to take my clothes off, burn them, take a shower, get away from here. I wanted to go home.

"Mrs. Ziegenmeyer," Deborah Smith said gently, "the police have to come into this. These men, they repeat this crime, over and over. The longer we wait, the better chance he has of getting away and doing the same thing he's done to you to someone else, to another woman like you. With your help, maybe we can stop him before that happens."

Stop him? I could stop him?

"All right," I said wearily. "Call the police. And I guess you can call the person from that center. Whatever."

"The rape crisis center. Polk County Victim Services."

Rape. Crisis. Victim.

"OK. And Steven, my husband. Somebody has to call Steven." But not me. I couldn't do it, not yet. "Steven's Aunt Doris lives in Des Moines," I told them. "I want to call her."

"OK," Beverly Clark said, "we'll do that. What's her number?"

I didn't know it, I couldn't remember it. It was in my address book. He—my rapist—had taken my address book. I gave her the last name, my best guess about the address, and the two of them went through the Des Moines phone book until they found Aunt Doris.

We made the call, and Uncle Gordon answered the phone. Aunt Doris had left for work, he said, but he'd find her, and they'd get to the hospital as soon as they could. Don't worry, he told me, we're on our way.

Almost immediately, it seemed, the person from the crisis center was standing there.

"Mrs. Ziegenmeyer? Nancy?" she said, and I looked up. She was blond, with kind eyes and the beginning of a smile on her face. It was a compassionate smile. She told me her name was Dee Ann Wolfe, and that she'd stay with me now, for the examination, for the police, for whatever I needed.

Then Deborah and Beverly walked me down the hall to an examining room. Dee Ann began to prepare me for the physical examination, helping me undress, patting my shoulder when I got rigid at her touch. And then Deborah gave me a hospital gown, and they helped me onto the table. I was cold, shaking uncontrollably, and my nose was running. I was shredding tissue after tissue in my hands, and Dee Ann just kept handing me another one.

The doctor, Dr. Kees—a woman, I was grateful to see—gently examined me as though I was glass that might shatter into a thousand pieces under her hands. Dee Ann stayed right next to me, standing at the head of the examining table, quietly explaining each step as the nurses and the doctor worked together.

They combed the hair on my head. They combed my pubic hair. They swabbed inside my mouth. They took skin from beneath my fingernails, then clipped them, including the poor little mangled one on my right hand. They took rectal smears and vaginal smears, marking swabs "A" and "B."

"We'll do tests on these, Nancy," said Dr. Kees. "There are ways now to identify him. And we have to make sure you're healthy, too." Healthy? Disease? He'd mentioned AIDS, something about me giving it to him. But what about him giving it to me? And VD? And syphilis? Herpes? There was no fear of pregnancy—I'd had to have a hysterectomy years before—but the diseases, my God, the list of possibilities was endless. In addition to everything else, could this man make me sick, too?

When the examination ended, I asked please, could I please take a shower? But they didn't have the facilities for that, the nurses said. Dee Ann gave me a warm, gray sweat suit, donated by her agency, to wear, since the hospital had to turn all my clothing over to the police to use as evidence. One of the waiting police had taken my car keys so they could go out and examine the car, dust for fingerprints, whatever else they might be able to find. And now they were waiting for me to give my statement. Aunt Doris and Uncle Gordon were waiting, too. But before I did anything else, I said, I had to call Steven.

Aunt Doris placed the call and then handed the receiver to me. It felt like a cold, ten-pound weight in my hand, and I couldn't get any words out once Steven had answered. Aunt Doris took the phone back and told him she was with me, we were at the hospital in Des Moines. At first he thought it was a car accident, a wreck, that maybe something had happened on the Interstate. But she said no, and handed me the phone again.

The tears really came then, huge shudders that made me stammer between words. I don't know how he understood me, but he did. All he wanted to know was, was I hurt, had I been injured?

"I'm sorry," I sobbed. "Please don't hate me. He made me do it, please forgive me. And the kids, he said he knew where we lived, he threatened to come after the kids. Please don't leave the kids!"

I was almost incoherent with fright. What if Steven came to the hospital to get me, leaving the children, and then my rapist went to our house before we got back home? Even if my mother was there with them, she would be no match for him. That man would get my kids.

It was finally decided that Steven would stay in Grinnell with the children; after I'd given my statement to the police, Aunt Doris and Uncle Gordon would take me home as soon as they could.

"We'll be right here," Steven said.

Dee Ann told me that it was now time for me to go into the conference room and talk to the police investigator who was going to make the report.

"I can't do it," I told her. "I can't tell this. I want it to be over, and if I tell it, it'll just go on and on. It's ugly, and I hate it. What if he doesn't believe me?"

How could I tell a man—for it was a man waiting for me in there, she'd told me that—what another man had done to me? How could I possibly get those words out, about what he did, and where he did it, and how he did it, and what he made me do? No, I couldn't.

"Yes, you can, Nancy," she reassured me. "The officer's name is Ralph Roth, and I've worked with him before. He's a friend, and he's been through this with other women who've been attacked. He's married, and he has daughters, and he's a nice man, a kind man. And maybe even more important, he's very good at what he does. If you don't tell Ralph, then we can't stop this guy."

Back to that again. Stopping this guy. OK, I told her, OK, and I walked into the conference room, dragging my feet and feeling as if I'd done something terribly wrong and now my punishment was coming.

At the table sat a man in glasses, a notepad and a pen in front of him. He wasn't wearing a uniform. He looked up at me and he had the same look on his face that Dee Ann had worn when she had first come into the examining room. This wasn't a garden party, after all, so nobody was grinning, but there was the beginning of a smile there, and there were lines around his mouth from where he'd smiled a lot.

My first reaction to Ralph was that he didn't look like anybody's idea—my idea, maybe, or TV's idea—of a big-deal, macho investigative cop. He looked like everybody's father.

"Mrs. Ziegenmeyer?" he asked, half rising from the chair, and he put out his hand. I put mine out, too, but pulled it back when I touched him. His voice was calm and warm. And there was a cigarette burning in the ashtray next to him. I pulled out a chair—it made an awful noise scraping across the floor—and sat down at the table. I looked down at my watch, my Wally World special. It was nearly 11:00 A.M. The test, I thought. I guess I'm not taking that test today. Crying again, or maybe still crying, I started to tell him the story. . . .

CHAPTER THREE

GOT A CALL about a sexual assault victim at Mercy Hospital
and arrived there about 9:00 A.M.," says Ralph Roth, who
in November of 1988 was a sexual abuse investigator in the
Des Moines Police Department's Crimes Against Persons section.

"When I got there, Mrs. Ziegenmeyer, Nancy, was still in
the examining room. It's sure as hell not my job to stick my
nose in there while that's going on, so we didn't actually begin
to talk until around 10:45, when she walked into the conference room with Dee Ann. I knew Dee Ann, we had worked
together before.

"I remember Nancy's chin was down to her chest. She's a
little person, only five-two or five-three, and the sweats were
bigger than she was. At that point, I think, she was pretty
apprehensive about men. It was hard, at first, to get her to look
at me when she was talking.

"I knew I had to establish right off the bat that I can never
walk in her shoes, but if she'll just give me the opportunity, if
she'll just talk with me, maybe I can get this investigation
going. I told her that I understood that she did everything
possible that she could've done, that I knew what had happened was degrading and that we—the police—didn't think
you had to have black eyes or scratches or be beat up or stuff
like that, just to be believed. She was crying then, saying 'He
made me do it, he made me do it.' I looked at her, her stature,

versus her description of the person that did this to her. Eventually you just have to give in, I told her. I said, Nancy, don't worry. You don't have to keep telling us. We know he made you do it.

"When I asked her if she minded if I smoked, I saw a little light go on in her eyes for the first time. She bummed a cigarette from me, and it wasn't the last one either. Her cigarettes had been in her bookbag.

"I had to take her back to the beginning, what she was doing in the city that day, where she was, what time this was. Had to make her go step by step.

"When she got to the actual rape, her head went down again, and her speech slowed way down. She wanted me to know she'd fought, she'd hollered. I think, when I talk to a lot of victims, they always feel as if there was something else that they might've done, something more. I try to reassure them, let them know that, hey, at least we're here today, now, and we're talking with each other, and that's the most important thing.

"When she told me about the pillar with the numbers on it, combined with the fact that she got a quick look at this guy, I began to feel good. That detail was a beginning, a place to start.

"She was roller-coastering up and down. I know, when I start hitting the pressure points, to slow down, back off, let them tell it in their own time. She wants to tell it, it's all right there, but every few minutes she'll get right up to it and it gets tense again.

"Dee Ann was with us, sitting right next to her, and it was one of those rooms where people need to come in and go out, another lady from the emergency room, hospital stuff. But little by little, it's just me and her. And I'm smoking, and she's smoking, and I'm watching her as she's getting stronger.

"She had good details, and a time frame that everything fits into. Once she'd gone through the story, picking up the details here and there, I told her we had to get right back out there, to the street, and see if we can go through it together.

"She says, 'Right now?' and her face locks up. And I know what she feels like. But she lives out of town, and I wanted to get as much from her as fast as I could.

"So we piled into the unmarked patrol car, me, her, Dee Ann, her Aunt Doris and Uncle Gordon. We started with the first parking lot, where he picked her up, at the college. She said that she never heard traffic whizzing by after that. A block over is one of the major streets in this town, and she would've heard noise if he had taken her there.

"Then she sees the parking lot where he left her off. That'll give me a chance to maybe talk to some neighbors. Maybe somebody saw something. She isn't sure how she got to the hospital from there, doesn't know street names, but she remembers which way she went. Go down this way, go that way, this street, that one. Little by little, she's defining the area herself.

"We do another quick tour, looking for the pillar with 1320, and we find one place that could be a possibility. She wants to hang in there, wants to keep it up, but it's getting close to three now, and she's tired and shaky. I want to get her on the road with her family, headed home.

"So here we have a starting point, an ending point, a neighborhood, and all the description she can give me. We have the stuff from the hospital exam. We went over the car with a fine-tooth comb, and it's clear we've got somebody who's been involved in crime before, because he knows not to leave prints, prints that are probably on file someplace. And he's probably been identified before, because he was so careful to keep her head covered. Plus he took those rings. They were made especially for her, she told me, by the jeweler in Grinnell.

"When I send her home, she's tired, beat. She doesn't think we'll ever get him. But I'm up, because I know how much she's given me. It's better than a running start, I tell her. We're really going to go someplace with this."

CHAPTER FOUR

W HEN STEVEN HUNG UP the phone after talking
with me at the hospital, he got the three children
dressed, fed them, and then drove them over to my mother's
place.

My mom, Betty Dillon, lives in a big trailer house about
five minutes from our house. She's been divorced from my
dad almost from the time I was born. My dad, remarried now,
lives in Cedar Rapids, but Mom never married again, and
she's always been within hollering distance of me.

When I was little, we lived with my grandparents on a farm
in Searsboro, Iowa (population, back in those days, around
sixty-five, and not much different now). Mom went into
town—Grinnell—to work every day, and she seemed to like it,
but back then, town didn't hold any appeal for me at all. I
thought the sun rose and set on that farm, sitting as it did out
in the middle of wide, rolling fields of corn and hay, and I
thought the same sun rose and set on my grandparents' heads.
I wanted to stay there with them always, and I grew up thinking that old houses and the land around them were the best,
most valuable things in the world.

The farm was a working farm then, with hired help during
harvest season, and big meals, with everyone around the table
three times a day.

There were three or four farms that bumped up next to each

other, and it was the kind of place where all of them bought, paid for, and shared the same hay baler. Everybody worked together, one farm at a time, until the haying was done.

Sometimes, on summer afternoons, I'd wander off to the railroad tracks that ran along the edge of the farm property. I'd put pennies down on the track and then wait for the trains to come along and flatten them into little copper discs. The trains would blast by me, pushing the hot wind into my face, and then they'd be gone. For a minute or two, the flattened pennies would be almost too hot to touch.

At home, there were rocking chairs in Gramma's parlor and on the porch, and chores for the kids to do, and whenever I got into trouble, Grampa would address me as "Young Lady" in his you're-in-the-soup-now voice, and I'd stop right in my tracks.

I try not to draw too pretty a picture, for I know there were hard seasons there, with cold, constant wind in the winter, frozen pipes that burst in the night, and engines that wouldn't turn over. In the summer there was heat that fried everything in its path, the machinery broke, things wouldn't grow. To idealize farmers, rather than respect what is real about their lives, is to insult them. But for the child I was then, it was heaven.

Steven's always said I was spoiled rotten out there, and he was right. I wasn't necessarily spoiled with an abundance of things, although I was never denied anything. But I was spoiled with a life that had order to it, spoiled with attention, the richness of many laps to crawl into, lots of people who loved me, who could always fix what was wrong and make me feel safe and special.

Mom and I never really got close until I fell in love with Steven and had children of my own. It was then I began to understand what life had been like for her all those years ago. I had been a bullheaded daughter, sure always that my point of view was the only one worth considering and that no matter what we were fighting about, she was wrong. Even now, we're not particularly mushy or demonstrative with each other, but we're finally friends. I trust her. And I've always known that my kids feel as safe and happy with her in her trailer as I ever did on the farm.

When Steven took the kids to Mom's that day, I'm sure it was as much to get comfort for himself as it was to tell her the news. I can only imagine what it must have been like for him to tell her what had happened, to put it into words for the first time himself, and hear those words coming out of his mouth. He stayed there through much of the afternoon, watching the clock. They had a couple of beers, she fixed the children some lunch.

They agreed that it would be best that the children stay there with her until I got home, until he and I had a chance to be alone together and gather our wits.

Aunt Doris drove me home from Des Moines in her car, and Uncle Gordon brought up the rear in my GrandAm. All the way home, I sat and stared out the window in some kind of stupor, watching the acres go by. When we turned into the driveway, Steven wasn't back from Mom's yet. I went straight into the house, Aunt Doris behind me, Steven coming in behind us maybe two minutes later. It was four or so, nearly dark.

Saying nothing, Steven held his arms out to me. I walked into them and put my head on his chest. I couldn't say anything to him, and he couldn't speak either. He just stood there and held me while I cried. I was vaguely aware that Aunt Doris and Uncle Gordon had driven away.

After a few minutes, Steven started to steer me to the couch, wanting me to sit down, but I shrugged him off. I suddenly, desperately, wanted a shower. All I could think of was washing the day off me.

I asked him to bring me my own old gray sweatshirt, the one that hung to my knees, stretched and worn soft by years of washing. Then I headed straight for the bathroom.

I pulled off the rape crisis center's sweat suit and left it in a lumpy pile on the floor, and stepped into the shower, turning the water on as hot as I could stand it.

At first I just leaned on the shower wall and let the water hit me. I looked down at my body, and cried and cried. And then I started to scrub, then rinse, then scrub, then rinse. If only I could've peeled the skin off, go down to the bones somehow. I don't know how long I was in there, but I know I stayed until the water ran cold. When it finally got icy, I got out.

Right after I got dressed, we went to my mother's to get the children. Her reaction is a blur to me now, although I remember she offered to keep them a little longer. But all I could think of was getting my kids out of there, getting them home. I couldn't bear that there was someone out there who had threatened to hurt them if I went to the police. I had to get them back under our roof as soon as possible.

I couldn't tell them what had happened—at that point, I couldn't have gotten any words out of my mouth that would have made any sense. But they knew something frightening had happened, and they looked scared. "I love you, Mommy," they said, as if those were magic words that might make whatever it was go away.

"I love you, too," was all I could manage in reply. I remember thinking, so this is what being "struck dumb" means. When I was a kid, and would read that line in a book, I always thought it meant that somebody got stupid all of a sudden. Now I knew better—the mouth goes to the brain for words, but the brain comes up empty.

At bedtime, I wouldn't let the children sleep in their own rooms. I was afraid someone was going to come into the house and get them, even though I knew, because he kept saying it over and over, that Steven would have killed anybody who had walked through the door at that point. But I had to have them where we could see them.

So while I sat huddled in the middle of our bed, Steven gathered up their blankets and pillows, and brought all three of the kids into our room. He helped them make nests on the floor, trying to get them to believe that this was going to be fun, sleeping on the floor in Mommy and Daddy's room.

Once they were all settled in, we watched as they fell asleep around us. They were so little: Nick not yet seven, Ben five, Sissy four.

But Steven and I, we didn't sleep, or if we did, it was a drift-off-and-snap-awake kind of sleep. I was too tired to cry anymore, and neither one of us had figured out a way to speak coherently. It was like the old language didn't work, and we hadn't had time yet to invent a new one.

So we just lay there, holding each other, listening to the small noises children make when they sleep. And then the morning finally came, and it was time to start our lives all over again.

Neither Steven nor I had ever been very good at hiding our feelings. If we were in a good mood, we'd laugh and grab each other, telling jokes (even dirty ones) and fooling around. If we were fighting, we'd yell and swear at each other, and stomp around the house. Doors might slam, a pot might thunk down hard on a counter. We both swear way too much, and we've never hidden anything from the children, none of this "ssshhh, the children will hear" stuff. We hadn't ever seen the point in acting like that.

So hiding what had happened from the kids was never an option for us. We knew we had to tell them the truth, or as much of it as we thought their minds would understand at that point. And we had to let them know that the sadness and tension that had suddenly moved into our house was not their fault, but someone else's.

We had already talked to them about strangers, about good touch and bad touch, and it was something that their schools were teaching them, too, so we already had the words to use to tell about such a hard thing.

We told them a man had touched Mommy bad, but that

Mommy had told the policeman, just like you're supposed to. Now the policeman was going to get that man and send him away to jail.

Big-eyed, they all gathered close around us, looking back and forth, first to me, then to Steven. They knew Mommy's feelings were hurt and that Daddy was really mad, and they looked totally bewildered. The boys tried to tough it out, but Sissy began to cry.

I hadn't ever wanted my children to think of the world outside our door as a scary place. They were open and friendly, just as I had been when I was little. I used to believe everybody, trust everybody, and I'd always believed that it was a good trait to pass on to my kids. Don't be afraid, I'd tell them. You can do anything you set your mind to, just get out there in the world and do it. There's nothing to be afraid of. Suddenly it seemed as if I hadn't known what the hell I'd been talking about.

To lose control over my own body, to have someone take that away, was bad enough. To lose my own sense of the world as a place of joy and possibility was somehow worse. That bastard had taken that away from me, and he'd taken it from my family. In essence, without actually killing me, he'd taken away my life. The hardest thing to do each day was facing that loss, and facing the same question over and over: How do I get my life back?

CHAPTER FIVE

THE TOWN WHERE WE LIVE is smack in the middle of the Iowa prairie, Exit 162 off Interstate 80, with a population that ranges between eight thousand and ten thousand, depending on whether or not Grinnell College is in session. The town was started in the mid-1800s by Josiah Bushnell Grinnell, a Vermont minister who supposedly was the "young man" on the receiving end of Horace Greeley's advice to go west. Reverend Grinnell set up shop at a railroad stop midway between Iowa City and Des Moines, breaking up his six thousand acres into lots for frame houses, churches, schools, and a park at the center. Every deed he issued contained a provision that the property would revert back to Grinnell if intoxicating liquor was sold on the premises. I suspect a lot of folks would be in line to lose their shirts if that provision was enforced these days.

An important object of the town's pride for more than a hundred years has been the college, a small (twelve hundred students) private liberal arts school that consistently ranks in the nation's top ten for its size. It was the first college west of the Mississippi to grant bachelor's degrees, and the first west of the Mississippi to host an intercollegiate football game.

In summer, the campus is like a green oasis at the town's heart, with its big brick buildings, its old trees shading the lawns and sidewalks, and the wonderful Victorian houses on every street, some of them in the National Register of Historic Places.

As in every small town, with its Main Street and its post office and its grocery stores where the checkout clerks see pretty much the same people week after week, it's difficult to be anonymous in Grinnell. The good part of that, of course, is that it's a healthy place to raise a family. If your child rides a bike down the street, the people at the other end of the street know who he is and where he lives. They might remember that he got the bike as a birthday present. They'll ask, if it's 11:00 on a midweek morning in April, why that boy isn't in school like he should be. Maybe they'll call you to inquire, or they might call the school—the odds are, they know the principal personally, and they may even know his teacher.

If that same boy runs a temperature, the doctor won't have to look down his throat or in the file to see if he's still got his tonsils—he'll remember taking them out himself, two years ago this spring. Your neighbors know you and you know your neighbors. If you need help, you don't have to yell very loud. Of course, if you *do* yell loud and you *don't* need help, they'll all speculate on just what the hell's going on at your house.

For days and days after the rape, I stayed home. I didn't have a job to go to, and wouldn't have gone if I did. I'd wake up in the morning in a fog, after a bad night's sleep. If I'd had to get up in the middle of the night to go to the bathroom, I'd wake Steven up, too—I was too scared to walk through the dark house alone. At first he came right into the bathroom with me. Then, after a few nights, he stayed just outside the door until I was ready to go back to bed.

Steven's a diesel mechanic at Grinnell Implement, a private dealership for Case International. He's worked there since he graduated from high school, nearly twenty years. It's not the kind of job that meant he could stay home for days on end and hold my hand. He had to get back to work, and I had to get used to being in the house alone. Oh, the children were there, but it was Steven who would stand between me and whatever terror was outside.

During the day, I'd jump if the phone rang, or if someone came to the door. At night, I'd jump if the wind rattled a window or blew a tree branch across the yard. Shadows scared me, and so did darkness, and noise, and silence. Maybe silence scared me the worst.

I stopped letting the children walk to and from school. I drove them there, or Steven would, and I'd pick them up afterward, although getting my courage up to leave the house and get into the car took at least ten to fifteen minutes every time. And once I got into the front seat, I was confronted with the wispy traces of white powder on the dashboard, where the police had dusted for prints. There was no question of selling the car—it had been practically brand new when I'd been raped, and we weren't in any position to be buying a new car just because the old one gave us the creeps. Besides, it was a nice car. I liked it. It was my car. Damn it, it was my car.

I couldn't shop for groceries. Steven would take the big list and go on Sundays, and Mom would get what I needed the rest of the time. I smoked too much, I took a lot of showers, and I either didn't eat at all or ate junk food. Nothing tasted very good. I didn't cook much, and that made me sad. I had always loved to cook.

Small things made me crazy. My glasses had been in that damn bookbag, and my contact lenses. And my makeup. Even if I had wanted to fix my face and show it in public, I couldn't, not without going out and buying all that stuff. My charge cards were in the bag, and my driver's license. My certificate for having completed the real estate course. My textbook, my notebook. And my address book, with telephone numbers I'd had for years. I might've thought, before this, that I'd had most of those numbers memorized. But I didn't. Each time I wanted to make a call, I had to look up the number, and by the time I got through looking it up, I'd usually decide I didn't want to make the call.

At first I didn't want to tell anyone about the rape. As the days passed, I told only the closest of our friends. I didn't want to talk about the details, and I dreaded being comforted, being touched, people reaching out to me, people looking at me. But there were some people I loved, who loved me, and they would have had to have been blind not to know that something godawful had happened, especially since only days before I had been on my way to being the world's most ambitious real estate salesperson.

It was so hard to tell our best friends, Ron and Diane Pickens. But I could never have kept this a secret from them. They are as close as family—closer, in the way friends sometimes become—and enough older than the two of us that I think of them as second parents. They have two grown daughters, and it was too easy for Ron and Diane to imagine how they would have felt if this had happened to them.

Some friendships are "like him, hate her." But this friendship was between the four of us, in all four directions. Steven says he's not afraid of anybody in the world—except Diane. And he and Ron have spent time together tinkering under the hood of the '57 Chevy Ron's restoring. They're the kind of friends that we saw a lot; we even went on trips out of town with them—and that can be the toughest test of friendship. When we go someplace together, Diane and I sit in the front (I'm always the designated driver, mostly because I'm the fastest) and Steve and Ron sit in the back, drinking their beer, making fun of my driving. The fall before, we'd gone on a riverboat ride down the Mississippi, and then Diane and I hit almost every antique shop in Dubuque. When I thought of that trip, it seemed as if it had happened years ago.

And we had to tell Penny and Randy Storbeck. Steven had gone to school with Randy, and I had baby-sat their towheaded baby, Little Randy, almost from the day he was born. He was as at home in my house as my own kids were, and Penny and I had spent hours at my kitchen table, ordering stuff from catalogs, drinking coffee, and solving the problems of the world. Penny had always said that if she and Randy were ever to split up, Steven might as well build another bedroom on our house—she was moving in.

And I told Cathy Burnham, whose house was on the street

behind ours. Her husband, Keith, had also gone to high school with Steven, and they have two little boys who play with ours. It was an over-the-back-fence friendship, based mostly on swapping kids for overnights, or when one couple or the other wanted to go out.

But the only person I really wanted to talk to was Dee Ann Wolfe, at Polk County Victim Services' Rape Crisis Center. Steven and I drove to Des Moines twice for group sessions, and Cathy Burnham went with me once, but it was too difficult to keep going. The meetings started at 5:30, which meant going to the city in rush-hour traffic and then driving home in the dark. So finally, I started calling Dee Ann on the phone two or three times a week. She was like a kind of lifeline to the world. She'd seen me at the very worst, that first morning in the hospital, and she'd taken my hand at that moment and it still felt, even though I was in Grinnell and she was in Des Moines, that she had never let it go.

Even after I'd started finding ways to keep busy around the house, with laundry or housework or cooking, there would come moments when I just stopped functioning, and the pictures of what had happened in the car would rush back into my head. It would feel as if he was coming in the front door, just walking in whenever he felt like it, and there was nothing I could do except shake and cry.

When the phone would ring, I'd just stand there and watch it. Penny would answer it for me if she was there, but otherwise, I'd just let it ring until whoever was on the other end finally gave up.

I'd have tremendous bursts of energy and maniacally scrub everything in sight, and the next day I'd be really down, tired and sleepy and barely able to talk.

I'd get so bitchy at the children, snapping at them for stupid things. Crayons not put back in boxes, socks left on the floor. And then I'd get weepy at the looks on their faces, and grab them, and hold them too tight, for too long, until they fidgeted and tried to wriggle away. And that would make me mad all over again. When they were bad, I took it personally. When they were good, I didn't notice. They wanted to understand what was going on, but if I didn't, how could I expect them to?

That's when I'd call Dee Ann, and she'd talk me through it. She probably heard the rendition of that day in hell a hundred times, with every sickening detail intact. Maybe, after we hung up, she yelled at her office walls in frustration with me, but if she did, she never let on. It seemed, some days, like her patience was bottomless.

The most important thing I started to learn during those early days was what rape is and what it is not. What it is not, I heard over and over, is sex. What it is, is violence. The man may use sex, his own and the victim's own, as a weapon against her, just like he'd use a gun: to frighten her, to dominate her, to threaten and to terrify. But ultimately, what had happened to me was an act of violence, not an act of sex. The struggle for most victims, I learned, was to separate out the two, and to try to remove self-blame and self-doubt from the equation entirely.

I would go over and over that morning, replaying it in my mind like a bad video. I should have remembered to lock the car door. I shouldn't have parked where there were no other cars. Maybe I shouldn't have gone there at all. Maybe I should've fought harder, screamed louder, broken all ten of my fingernails and a couple of my bones.

That was the most destructive kind of thinking, and soon enough I realized that I could what-if myself until hell froze over and never change what happened. And then I would hear Dee Ann's voice: Nancy, you didn't do anything wrong. *He* did.

I became absolutely fixated on the crisis center's sweat suit. I had washed it, and folded it, and put it away neatly, but then I decided I just had to get the damn thing out of the house. When I called Dee Ann and asked her how could I get it back to her, she told me that it was mine to keep.

"I don't want it," I said, and then hounded Steven for days until he took it to the Goodwill store.

I know I wasn't the only woman Dee Ann was helping, but I never felt that I was just a number on her long list. When I talked to her, and swore, and cried—sometimes sobbing so much I couldn't continue—I always felt that what I said was important, that who I was, and how I was, mattered to her. Learning to trust her was, in many ways, like learning to walk all over again.

Sometimes the feelings I had inside scared me, they were so wild. There were days when I was sure I was simply going to slide into total craziness and never come back. Who was this guy, I'd sob, and *where* was he? And Dee Ann would come back on the other end of the line, saying no, Nancy, you're not going crazy. When I thought I wasn't getting over it fast enough, she said no, no, there's no timetable on this, no clock ticking off what's a long time, what's a short time, what's an appropriate time. You have to take your own time.

Worse than my fear of the rapist suddenly appearing on my doorstep was my fear that I would lose Steven. Oh, sure, in my head I could wrestle with the idea of rape as violence, and maybe begin to get it through to my brain that what had happened had nothing to do with my sexual relationship with my husband. But getting the message through to my heart was another battle. Our sex life had always been very important to me, and to us as a couple. It might've been the place where the anger and frustration got played out during our bad times, but it had mostly been a source of great joy. We had resolved fights in that bed. A few times, we had laughed so hard we had almost fallen out of that bed. Most important, we had made our babies in that bed.

I know now, from the women I've talked to and all the reading that I've done, that it's sometimes weeks or months or even years before victims feel healed enough to begin again in a sexual relationship, no matter if it's with a new partner, or an old, familiar, well-loved one.

But for me, it was different. I was afraid that if I waited for healing (and who could guarantee that I would heal at all?) I would lose my husband and lose myself in the bargain. I didn't know if he could love me again, and I didn't know if I could let him.

I needed to find out, as a woman, as a person, that with all the rapist had taken from me, he hadn't succeeded in taking away what Steven and I had shared. And I needed to know it as soon as possible.

So that Sunday night, one day after the rape, I asked him to make love to me. Without hesitation, he did. We watched each other closely, Steven looking for my fear or pain, me looking for his revulsion or rejection. Step by step, as we cautiously moved through something that used to be dearly familiar, he'd stop and ask if I was OK.

It was not the best sex we'd had in our nine years together, but that wasn't what I was looking for. What I *was* looking for, I found.

It became increasingly obvious that any idea I might have had of going back to real estate was out: The very thought of walking into an empty house with a stranger made me sick to my stomach, and I didn't see how that was ever going to change. But the need for a second income was still there. Working nights again, in a restaurant or a bar, was completely off the list of possibilities now. What could I do?

Steven and I talked and talked, and we finally decided that I could start a little baby-sitting service, and take children into our house.

For one thing, we had an old place that could absorb the wear and tear: After all, we had three wild ones of our own, finger-painting on the dining room table, or banging away on the piano. What serious difference would it make if there were five or six more? We had a yard big enough for the sunny days, and I knew very well what it was like to entertain a house full of noisy, fidgety children when it was raining outside. And kids were about the only people left who didn't scare me. They'd keep me busy, which I needed now more than ever. Most important, I wouldn't have to leave the house.

Within a day or two after our decision, I'd made enough phone calls and talked to enough people to bring in six children. I didn't know if I would do it long term—I couldn't even think long term, about this or anything else—but it would solve our problem for now.

Through it all, we were living one day at a time, some days good, some days godawful. Thanksgiving had gone by in a gray blur, and the commercials on TV squawked Christmas was coming, Christmas was coming, and everywhere I looked were reminders that someplace out there was an ideal life, where people were safe and everybody was smiling. I might as well have revived my childhood belief in the tooth fairy as try to believe that kind of life was possible now for us. Especially since also out there was the man who raped me.

I was haunted by the fact that the man could've killed me. But he didn't, and once I'd had time to think about that, it became scarier and scarier. Life wasn't just *there* anymore. It was something that needed to be dealt with, to be taken care of, and not to be taken for granted.

For instance, I hadn't even realized, in any conscious way, that my Grampa and Gramma weren't always going to be around. Steven and I used to fight about it sometimes. He'd say, "These people aren't gods, Nancy, they're not going to live forever." And then I'd get pissy at his insistence that I be a grown-up. Be realistic. And now, here realism was, right in my face, in all its ugliness. And the ugliness was all I could see. I knew this was no way to live, but I was stuck, and couldn't get out of my own way.

Where was the system, I wondered? Where were the people who were supposed to be on my side, who would find the person who'd blown up my life? And what about that detective, Ralph Roth—had he just turned me into a file folder, stuck in the middle of all the other file folders on his desk? I wanted to believe he was still going up and down the streets of Des Moines, looking for the rapist. And I wanted to believe he wouldn't stop until he got him.

CHAPTER SIX

W E'RE UP TO THE FIRST of December by now," says Detective Roth, leaning way back in his office chair and glancing only sporadically at his notes. He likes this story—and he knows it by heart. "Since I sent Zieg—I'd started calling her Zieg—back to Grinnell, we'd tried to expand the street-by-street search for the house with the damn pillar with the damn numbers on it.

"I check the East/West streets, the North/South streets, anything with a 1300 combination in it. Made me nuts. Drive up and down for hours, go to 1320, then 1230, then 1302. But she was so sure of 1320 that I decided I had to stay with that, and not doubt her.

"We get some information from Grand View College security that there was a suspicious black guy in that neighborhood driving a certain car, but that's fuzzy and doesn't pan out. I decide to focus on the rings.

"We have a system here that, anything that's pawned, because of the city ordinance, these people have to present identification, with addresses, with social security numbers. If they're leaving the stuff in pawn, the odds are that the information the pawn shop owners have is correct.

"So I spoke to the detective who monitors this, to find out if there's any way to find a particular set of rings pawned anywhere from say, the nineteenth of November through the current date. He explained that even if he had them on his printout, the descriptions would be very vague: one diamond ring, one white-gold band, like that. I said I didn't care, punch 'em up. He gave me about seven different places to check out. Even if the guy had taken the stone out, maybe we could still track the band.

"Sure enough, the second place I go to, there they were. I looked at them very hard, then went and checked out the other shops just to make sure, then came back. I was sure. Reason is, a girl named Lisa Davis pawned them on November 21, about 1:30 in the afternoon. The rape happened on the nineteenth, a Saturday. The shop was closed on the twentieth, a Sunday. First chance to pawn the rings? Monday. Another thing was, Zieg was picked up and then left back in the 1000 block of Boyd Street. This lady, Lisa Davis, shows her address at 1423 Boyd.

"I call Nancy, she tells me her rings are size seven. I go back to the pawn shop and have the guy check them out on the ring sizer. Sure enough, size seven. At this point, I confiscate them and tell my boss I had to take them to Grinnell.

"I drive out there the next day, thinking could this be? Or not? Could be, could not be, like Ping-Pong in my head. When I get to her house, Zieg's there all by herself. 'What have you got?' she asked over and over. 'What have you got?' I said, 'Look at these,' and roll the rings out of the envelope and onto the kitchen table. And she knows they're hers. She picks them up, looking for the flaw in the band that's always been there. And she finds the flaw.

"She's bouncing around the room, and she calls Steve. He comes right home and says yes, those are the rings. They told me the jeweler, who'd made the rings especially for her, could confirm the identification. So we get in the car and go there, to have him take a look. Hammond's Jeweler. What a nice man.

"Zieg's not thrilled, though, because I have to take the rings back to Des Moines. She can't have them back yet—they're evidence.

"Then we swing by the Grinnell Police Department and get

fingerprints, Nancy's and Steve's, because we've found a single print in the car and we don't know whose it is. This is on a Friday—by Monday, I find out the print is Nancy's. That's OK with me, at least we won't get it thrown back at us in court later, as some kind of ghost print that could point to somebody other than our guy.

"On December 6, I go to 1423 Boyd, and a man opens the door. I'm looking for Lisa Davis, because that's who pawned the rings, but I bullshit this guy for a little, pardon my French, saying I meet so many people on my job that I need to know who he is, how I can get hold of him during the day, and so on. His name is Bobby Lee Smith, he says, and he's employed at the Youth Emergency Shelter, where he counsels kids.

"Smith tells me that Lisa Davis isn't there, she's at her mother's. He gives me another address, and I head over there, but Lisa's not there either. The woman there says Lisa doesn't live there, she lives at the other address, with Smith. I go back, give him my card, and ask him to ask Lisa Davis to give me a call. Then I decide to go down to this Youth Emergency Shelter to see what I can find out about this person I just talked to.

"See, there had been another rape, a young woman from Indianola, a couple of days prior to Nancy's, and the description of the attacker had been the same. This guy, Bobby Lee Smith, I'm looking at him, I'm thinking . . . well, I didn't want to call it absolutely, but I was thinking maybe, just maybe . . . and I finally remember this guy, from back when he was on the local high school athletic teams. He was pretty good back then.

"So I go to the shelter. It's a private agency, contracted by the Department of Human Services, and I talk to this lady, who's evidently his boss. I tell her who I was. She says, 'Don't you know about Bobby?' Turns out he's on parole. I ask if I can see Smith's time card, so she gives me the record of each and every day and time he'd worked. Sure enough, when he punched in and out shows the right time frame—he could've easily been involved in both attacks.

"So I come back here with the information and run a criminal history on Smith. He has a record back to 1982. Third-degree theft, two years' probation. Carrying weapons in 1985, $200 fine. And second-degree robbery in 1987, with a ten-year prison term. He's on parole for that one.

"I get a call later that day from Lisa Davis, who's gotten my message. I explain why I'd been at the house—because of the rings she'd pawned on November 21. And she says to me right off the bat, 'What's that lady trying to say?' And I said, 'What lady? What are you trying to tell me?'

"Then she launches into this story, she had the rings three weeks before she pawned them. She'd been at a convenience store at Fourteenth and Hull, she said, and this Hispanic couple, Mexican, she says, was there. They had a little black car, and they couldn't get it started. They either needed a jump or gas, Lisa wasn't sure, but they had no money, and this lady takes her rings off and gives them to Lisa Davis. In return, Lisa Davis gives them ten dollars and a telephone number to call, so that when they can pay back the ten dollars, she can give them back the rings.

"I think about that for about half a minute. No woman, it seems to me, unless you're down to your last . . . well, you wouldn't give away your wedding rings. And she's telling me this happened three weeks before? Couldn't have been. Got the rings, got Nancy, got the jeweler's ID. Now I've got this lady telling me when she got 'em, when she pawned 'em. This is just bullshit.

"The next day, I drove back to Grinnell, with a photo spread for Nancy to look at. They're not candids, they're booking shots, each matted in a sort of window. I always use six at a time. Nancy looks at them, picks out Bobby Lee Smith's, then says could be, could be, but she's only half sure. She asks if there might be a more recent picture of him?

"At this point I think I've got to get him [Smith] into the police department. When I got back to Des Moines, I called him, said I needed to talk to him. About what, he wants to know, hemming and hawing and getting all defensive. Next thing I know, I've got his parole officer in here wanting to know what I'm all about. I tell him I want Bobby in here, to read him his rights. The parole officer said OK, he'd get him to cooperate, that would be the fastest way we could clear this up.

"The way we left it was, Bobby would come into the department the next day, voluntarily, and stand in a lineup. Then I call Steve and Nancy and ask them to come in. And I also call the other young woman, the other victim, to come in at the same time.

"The next day, Nancy and Steve come into the police department, and Dee Ann's with them. And so we're standing around and waiting, and everybody's pretty jumpy, and we get a phone call from Bobby.

"He says he can't come in, because he's talked to his attorney, and he gives me the guy's name. His attorney's sick that day, he says, and can't come in with Bobby, and he doesn't want to be there without representation.

"After I hang up, I check back with this attorney's office, and they don't remember a Bobby Lee Smith calling. He must've pulled the guy's name out of a hat. Anyway, so much for that.

"Then in comes the other young woman, the one from Indianola, with her rape crisis counselor, Harold Welles. And I say, the whole thing's off, Harold, my guy's not coming in. Then I tell him it's Bobby Lee Smith, and he says, 'But I know him! And I just saw him! He was just downstairs in this building!'

"Turns out, Bobby had made his call to me from the pay phone right downstairs. All I could think of was, what if either of these women had seen him down there? Or Steve? And Steve's really seething at this point, he probably would've gone after him!

"We decide then to do the next best thing, which is find the Polaroid in Bobby's file that was taken the last time he was booked. It's a closeup, three-way view, a regular mug shot. I separate the women and have them each take a look at this picture. Boom, the Indianola woman says, 'That's him.' Boom, Nancy says, 'That's him. That's absolutely him.'

"So that's it. I've got the time frame, and the rings linked to the girl he lives with, and the two solid identifications, and Bobby can't account for his time. He tells me, well, maybe I could've been playing basketball. . . . So I called the county attorney.

"December 8, we get an arrest warrant for kidnapping in the first degree. Built into that is the sexual assault charge. In Iowa, that's as bad as it gets. mandatory life sentence, no parole

"We also get a search warrant for the house. We'd found out that there had been a trash fire at Bobby's on the day Nancy was attacked. Sometime that afternoon, the fire department had come and put out a fire in a barrel. I kept thinking, he took everything from her in the car, maybe he burned it. Or maybe he's left something lying around his house. Plus, Nancy had described the suit he was wearing, so we take two suits out of his closet, similar to the ones she'd described. And the sweat socks . . . he's an athlete. White sweat socks, that's all he's got.

"When we first get there, Bobby asks us why we're there. When I tell him, he calls Lisa. She gets home and sees the warrant. Why are you arresting him, she wants to know. I explain the charges, thinking maybe the words 'sexual assault' or 'rape' will get some kind of reaction out of her. But nothing. Then I ask her, point-blank, what you're telling me about how you got the rings, you're not leaving anything out? But she sticks to it. So I arrested her right there, as an accessory after the fact.

"While we're taking Bobby to jail, he gets very talkative, very inquisitive, wanting to know dates, times, who identified what. He was trying to get me to give up the information. He says something, I don't remember what exactly, about white women. He was just out shooting some hoop, he says to me, why are these people doing this to him?

"When we get him there, since I also have a warrant for his body samples, the medical technician came over. Bobby understands at that point he has to give these things, he has no problem with it. Hair, saliva, blood samples, and so on.

"His minister comes down to talk to me, then his boss, his parole officer, all wanting to know how such a thing could've happened. I keep hoping Bobby Lee Smith will give himself away somehow. But he goes into Mr. Calm, Mr. Cool.

"A few days after New Year's we get another court order, from Nan Horvat, the assistant Polk County attorney. She's taken pictures of Zieg's rings, and the pictures will be used as evidence. Zieg can have her rings back."

CHAPTER SEVEN

W HEN RALPH BROUGHT my rings to Grinnell the first time, I began to have hope: hope that we'd find out who did this to me, hope that there would be a trial and the man would be punished, hope that a trial and a verdict would somehow end this bad dream that I woke up into every day. If I could put those rings on my finger, maybe they would work like a kind of magic, to somehow take me back to who I was before. And there was something about Ralph himself that made me think I could start to believe.

But then, when he took the rings back to Des Moines with him, the hope faded a little. Those rings were a symbol of my life with Steven. To see them shining on my kitchen table, and then watch them go back to Des Moines, with a police officer, to have them sit in a storeroom and be marked as evidence . . . well, that's it, I thought. I can't have my rings, and we'll never get the guy that did it, and that's all there is to it.

The next week Ralph brought some pictures to Grinnell to show me, and one of the men looked like he could've been the man who attacked me. The resemblance was so close—it was like seeing someone out of the corner of your eye. It was frustrating not to be able to say for certain, but I knew it was too important to risk making a sloppy identification.

A couple of days after that, Ralph called and asked would I

please come to Des Moines for what he called a one-on-one. I thought it might be something like the lineups I'd seen on television. The thought of actually seeing this person again, even in a police station . . . well, I took Steven with me, and Dee Ann met us there.

It turned out that the guy didn't show up. When it also turned out that while we had all been waiting in Ralph's office, the guy had been downstairs in the very same building the whole time, I dug my fingernails into Dee Ann's hand so hard I left a set of little red half-moon prints in her palm.

Once we realized that a lineup wasn't going to happen that day, Ralph rummaged around in his files and put together another set of mug shots. When he handed them to me, I got all cold and clammy. I'd seen this face too many times in my dreams not to be absolutely sure this time. My hands trembled as I held the pictures. No question this time—it was the man.

For legal reasons, Ralph had to keep me separated from the young woman from Indianola—he didn't want the court to say we had compared notes, or that we had somehow conspired to make the same identification. In some ways, I wanted to talk to her, to comfort her, to be comforted by her. Misery loves company, I guess. Maybe we couldn't talk, but when Ralph told me that she had made the same identification I did, it was as though we'd actually reached out to each other.

Ralph said he now had to get a warrant for the man's arrest, and there wasn't really anything else we could do here, although once he'd heard the guy had actually been downstairs, Steven came up with a few creative ideas of what *he'd* like to do.

When we left Ralph's office and turned down the hall, I came to an abrupt halt. Ahead of us way down the hall was a wooden bench, pushed up against the wall. Sitting on it were two black men. Without getting a closer look, I panicked.

"I think it's him," I said, grabbing Steven with one hand and Dee Ann with the other. "I can't go down there."

Ralph casually strolled down the hall and took a good look

at them, then just as casually strolled back to where we were standing.

"It's not him, Zieg," he said. "Come on, I'll walk you guys all the way to your car."

As Steven and I drove home, we talked about how we knew we had done all we could, that the rest was up to the police, and to the courts. We just had to go back and wait it out. We had, after all, a house full of kids (three of whom were our own) and the Christmas holidays to contend with. 'Tis the Season, and all that stuff.

Sometimes it really made me laugh, the way I'd started thinking in clichés: Misery loves company. Do the best you can. Look for the silver lining. One day at a time. Light at the end of the tunnel. Life goes on. Shit happens.

But Christmas had always been too special, we said, to let anyone or anything spoil it for us, or for the kids. I'd felt this way since I was little, and felt it even more now that I had a family of my own. I had always liked the baking, the music, and the kids' recitals at school. I liked the lights all over town. I liked the way the tree looked just before we decorated, and the way it looked afterward. I loved making lists for presents, shopping for them, wrapping them, then stashing them all over the house where Steven and the children couldn't find them. Best of all, always, was taking the family and going out to the farm on Christmas Day for dinner with Gramma and Grampa and the rest of the family.

This year, I wanted all these things more intensely than ever before. Some days my nerve endings seemed to be hanging like thread outside my skin. One verse of "Silent Night" was all it took, and I'd start crying. Even the kids singing "Jingle Bells"—and singing it badly—made my eyes tear up.

So one afternoon, Steven and I drove into Des Moines, to Toys-R-Us, to shop for the children's presents. I felt my heart rate speed up as we turned into the parking lot. Too many people, too much light, too much noise. Once we got into the building, it was pretty clear that the drill was going to be: get in, get it done, and get out as fast as possible. The aisles were full of people, pushing and pulling and bumping into each other. Their voices were raised, and everyone looked as crazy as I felt. We did the best we could with our list, and then we fled for home.

I had made one major decision that would make this holiday different from past years, and it had to do with a part of our family history that had been painful for years. It grew out of my realization—and again, here came the clichés—that life was short, that time runs out, that anything can happen. I had decided to invite Steven's parents, Charles and Wilma Ziegenmeyer, to our house during the holidays.

They wouldn't have to travel far—they only live five minutes from us. Yet for the last few years, it could've been the distance between earth and Mars for all the difference it had made to me.

My mother-in-law hadn't liked me from the day Steven first brought me home to meet her, and had rarely, if ever, bothered to hide her feelings. I was a junior in high school then—Steven was six years older—and I wasn't what she had planned for her son.

He had taken me to his parents' house one afternoon after work. We were going to go out that night, so I stayed in the living room while Steven went to shower and clean up. Wilma passed our first few minutes together by telling me all about Steven's ex-girlfriend and how wonderful she was. She even took out some magazine pictures of a wedding cake, and told me that this was the cake Steven and this wonderful girl were supposed to have had at their wedding. I might've been a kid, but I wasn't stupid, and it didn't take a rocket scientist to know this lady didn't like me one damn bit.

Two years later, when we were married, I was three months pregnant, which didn't do anything to endear me to Wilma. It only confirmed what she'd already decided: I had trapped him. From then on, my cooking, my clothes, the way I raised my children: nothing escaped her criticism.

Once, when Steven and I had been looking at a house to buy—our first—he decided to ask his dad to take a look at it. We drove to his folks' house, and Charles was out in the front yard. Steven asked him if he could jump in the car right then, Charles said yes, and they dropped me off and took off down the road. He didn't intend a slight to his mother, he just wanted the two of them to go take a look at the house alone, maybe take a look at the foundation, or the roof—the equivalent, I guess, of guys kicking the tires on a car they're thinking of buying. More than anything else, Steven wanted his father's company, and his father's opinion.

When I walked into the house and explained where they'd gone, Wilma flew into a rage, saying it was my fault Steven wasn't confiding in her. She blamed me for driving a wedge between them, saying I did it on purpose.

Another time, when I was hugely pregnant with Ben (I think I delivered him the next week, as a matter of fact), we were all at the funeral home to pay our respects to Steven's Grampa Stoker, Wilma's father. Suddenly Wilma took my arm and half-steered, half-dragged me up to the front of the room, right up to the open casket.

I don't know why she thought it was so important for me to get such a closeup look, but she kept a viselike grip on my arm and made sure I got an eyeful before she let go. The floor started to tilt beneath my feet, and I was sure the walls were coming in on us. It was sheer, claustrophobic terror, a chill, and an odd, blue crystal light somewhere way in the back of my brain. What I felt that day, standing in front of Grampa Stoker's casket, was exactly what came over me years later, trapped in the car with Bobby Lee Smith. I wanted to shriek like a little kid and run out of the room, but Wilma was hanging on to me, and I could feel people watching us. I was supposed to be a grown-up now. I stayed where I was.

Some people aren't afraid of dying, or of being around death. Wilma, for instance, says things like, "I've made my peace with the Lord, he can take me anytime." And I know other people who feel the same. Maybe their faith in God gives them that courage, or the kind of religious upbringing they've had, or maybe it's just something they're born with. Not me. I'm scared (I almost said "scared to death") of the whole thing, my own death and anybody else's, especially people I love, and I'm not afraid to admit it.

I had started out wanting Wilma to like me, hoping we could be friends. Steven knew her better than I and, even all those years ago, he strongly advised me to just forget about it. The great friendship, he had said sarcastically, was never going to happen.

So Steven would spend time with his father, and we'd see his two brothers and their wives, but gradually, Wilma wasn't part of the mix. Over the years there was one incident after another, some of them silly, some of them with serious consequences, until months would go by without Wilma and I speaking to each other. It had been Aunt Doris and Uncle Gordon who told the Ziegenmeyers about the rape, the day they brought me back home. The rumors of what Wilma's reaction had been were too ugly for me to believe.

But this Christmas I had simply decided that no matter what the history had been, no matter who had done what to whom, it was time to close the breach. They were Steven's parents, grandparents to my children. Bearing grudges took more energy, at that point, than I had in me.

They were surprised by the invitation, but they came to the house, bringing Christmas presents for the children and looking very nervous. The grown-ups were all a little stiff—we might've been better off if we'd broken out the liquor and actually *gotten* stiff—but the evening passed without a scene. I stayed on the sidelines, playing quiet hostess, and watched as they enjoyed the children's company. After they'd gone, I relaxed a little, thinking that was maybe the beginning of a change for all of us.

The hardest day was Christmas itself, and Christmas dinner, for although I'd looked forward to going to the farm, I had to face my grandparents' sorrow and consternation at what had happened to me. They'd had a good life, and a marriage of more than fifty years. It was completely beyond their imagining that this kind of thing happened in the world, and that it happened to their Nancy Jo. In addition to all the other havoc my rapist had let loose on this family, he'd made my grandfather feel helpless to protect me, and he'd made my grandmother cry.

After we had all exchanged gifts, I watched the platters of food being set on the table and saw the light in the children's eyes. All I wanted was a new year and the end of 1988, the worst year of my life.

CHAPTER EIGHT

O<small>N</small> J<small>ANUARY</small> 12, 1989, Bobby Lee Smith was arraigned in Polk County District Court on charges of kidnapping in the first degree. Bond was set at $100,000, which he couldn't pay. So he remained in jail, to my relief. The trial was set for March 15.

As the winter wore on, I had started heading for the Grinnell College library whenever I had the time. It seemed to me that there was so much I needed to know. I'd only been a so-so student in high school, and hadn't gone to college, so nothing had prepared me for being in the middle of the American justice system. It was like taking a crash course in language: police language, doctor language, lawyer language, and to further confuse me, science language, for studying DNA, the science of "genetic fingerprinting."

Nan Horvat, the assistant Polk County attorney, would be prosecuting what I had come to think of as "my" case against Bobby Lee Smith. She had told me that this new science had been used successfully as a "forensic tool" to identify rapists in other cases, and had been used once before in Polk County.

DNA (deoxyribonucleic acid) is a substance contained in every human cell. For a laboratory analysis, the materials that technicians can use are blood, semen, tissue and bone, saliva and bloodstains, urine, fingernails, and the roots of hair. And no two human beings—unless they are identical twins—have the same DNA.

All the physical evidence from my body, collected during the hospital examination, had been sent to the FBI laboratories in Quantico, Virginia, along with the samples they'd taken from Bobby Lee Smith. The preliminary information from the lab tests, Nan said, seemed to indicate that there were traces of Smith's DNA contained in my samples. In clearer language: His semen was found in my vagina.

But this technology, and the introduction of it as evidence in a rape trial, was still in its early stages and was considered very controversial, Nan warned me. Up until now, the testing had only been done by one or two private laboratories—our case was one of the first that had gone to the FBI's lab. Only a handful of experts in the entire country really understood how DNA testing and matching worked. But that didn't stop me from reading and reading in the library, trying to understand in weeks what it had taken professionals years to learn.

I'd never had anything to do with a criminal court proceeding, but this case was "my" case, and as the March trial date approached, I wanted to inform myself, teach myself, to be the best participant I could be. I began to keep a notebook with newspaper clippings and magazine stories about sexual assault victims. I collected statistics: Who were the victims, and what happened to them afterward? What happened to their attackers? Why did rape happen, and where, and how? I still made my phone calls to Dee Ann Wolfe for comfort and support, but increasingly, I was pumping her for information. Each source led to another, or two more, or three more.

I had a new address book now, with a collection of addresses and phone numbers that was growing more and more bizarre. The Iowa Crime Commission. The National Institute of Justice. The Project on the Status and Education of Women. The National Center for the Prevention and Control of Rape. The National Victim Center. If asked (and often if not asked), I could spout rape statistics broken down by region, population, arrests per age, per race, and per criminal. The more digging I did, the angrier I got.

At home, the terrible dreams continued. Some nights I

kicked Steven and thrashed around so much he had to get out of bed and go sleep on the couch. Other nights he'd wake to my pummeling him in the face. I'd be yelling, or crying, and he'd wake me up, literally yanking me out of the middle of the dreams.

But the days were busy and full, caring for my own children, caring for other people's children. I'd bake cupcakes and take them to the kids' classes if it was someone's birthday, and I'd take my turn reading at Story Hour at the school. But I would always take my notebooks along with me. They were getting thicker and thicker, and I liked looking at them. They were evidence that I was doing something. And a hefty chunk of my grocery money was being converted into dimes for the college copying machines.

"This is your final notice," the letter announced. "Unless paid in full immediately, we will place your account with our collection agency."

The amount owed was $600.80 for emergency services at Mercy Hospital Medical Center, for November 19, 1988.

Even at our poorest, Steven and I had never made a habit of ignoring bills. But we were damned sure going to ignore this one. I knew from my library research that Iowa state law said, "the cost of a medical examination for the purpose of gathering evidence and the cost of treatment for the purpose of preventing venereal disease shall be borne by the state Department of Health."

On advice from Bill Olson, our lawyer, I had called the billing department of the hospital and informed them of this fact, but they seemed slow to get the message. I was prepared to hold my ground. Maybe Iowa couldn't have prevented the attack on me, but I had no problem with expecting it to pick up the hospital tab.

Toward the end of February I was called to Des Moines to give my deposition, in the grand jury room of the Polk County

Courthouse. In the transcript of my deposition, it says, "Nancy Ziegenmeyer was called as a witness by the defendant." A witness. Called by the defendant.

It was then that my status in all of this began to sink in. I wasn't the plaintiff, the state of Iowa was. It wasn't my case, it was the state of Iowa's case. And from here on, in every official document that was created around this case, I would not be referred to as the victim, or the survivor, or even the rapee. I was just a witness.

Nan Horvat had tried to prepare me for this day, explaining where the deposition would be given, how the room would be set up, where we would all sit. We met in her office: Steven, me, Ralph, and, since Dee Ann couldn't be there with me, another woman, Karen, from the crisis center. As we all walked down the marble halls of the renovated courthouse toward the grand jury room, I could feel my feet dragging on the tile. I knew he was in there.

It didn't help to find out that Steven and Ralph had to stay out in the hall and wait until the deposition was finished.

"I don't think I can go in there," I said to them.

"Yes, you can, Nancy," Steven said, his voice flat. He was looking at the door. "You have to. We'll be right out here."

The room was no bigger than my kitchen. We arranged ourselves around the large conference table: the court reporter at the end, to my right, then me, then Nan. Karen was not allowed to sit at the table itself, but instead sat in a chair directly behind me. I promptly put my hand around behind my back and wriggled it through the wooden bars of my chair, where Karen grabbed it. That angled my body slightly away from the other side of the table, where John Wellman, from the public defender's office, sat.

Mr. Wellman is blind, so next to him was a young woman to assist him, a paralegal from his office, and next to her was Bobby Lee Smith—almost directly across from me, just two or three chairs down. Behind him, at some distance, stood a sheriff's deputy, in a uniform and armed with a gun.

Nan Horvat had told me that John Wellman had a fine reputation in Des Moines. He was considered ethical, even kind, and she said he probably wouldn't come at me like the defense attorneys I'd seen on television. Her reassurances, though, were of small comfort once he began, with quiet determination, to drag detail after detail out of me. He mercifully skipped over the actual sex parts, but that did nothing to ease what I was feeling.

Although I'd told the story often enough—to Ralph, to Steven, to Dee Ann, to friends and family—this time was different. Bobby Lee Smith was actually there. I never looked directly at him, we never made eye contact. But I knew he was right there, right outside the corner of my eye, listening to every word I said, taking notes on the legal pad on the table in front of him.

At some point, the sheriff's deputy evidently decided he had to head for the men's room. Without interrupting the proceedings, he just walked out. It suddenly occurred to me that I was now in a room with four women, a blind man, and the man who'd raped me. I had to bite my tongue to keep from blurting, "Holy shit!"

"May I take a break, please?" I said instead.

"Sure, anytime you want," said Mr. Wellman. I was already halfway across the room.

As I went out through the door, I ran head-on into Steven coming in. He'd seen the deputy leave the room, and decided there was no way I was going to stay in there without him.

When we got out into the hall, I took huge, gulping drags on a cigarette. It felt as if I'd just left a burning building, and I didn't want to go back in.

"Come on, you can do this, Zieg," said Ralph. Steven was cleaning his nails with his big pocket knife, and he looked at me and nodded. His face was contorted in a way I hadn't seen before. Sending me back in there alone was as hard on him as it was on me.

I couldn't believe, as Wellman's questions went on and on,

that there wouldn't come a moment when all of a sudden Bobby Lee Smith would just leap to his feet and yell, "All right! I did it, I did it!" I don't know why I waited for it to happen, but I did. I guess I wanted some reaction from him, some acknowledgment of me. But there was none. He kept his head down, and he kept taking notes.

I had to take one more break before we finally finished up. I'd gotten weepy again in the middle of telling the story, and I desperately wanted another cigarette. My shoulders ached, my arm was stiff from the position in which I'd held it, hanging on for dear life to Karen's hand. My nose was running and my eyes stung. I wanted to get out of that room and as far away from Bobby Lee Smith as I could.

And I was getting pretty damned tired of crying. I'd been called a lot of things in my life, but "wimp" had never been on the list. Yet for four, nearly five months, it seemed that all I ever did was cry. I was sick of it. Once the trial is behind us, I said to Steven that afternoon as we drove back to Grinnell, I planned to quit this crying, and put this whole mess behind us for good.

CHAPTER NINE

I LEARNED ABOUT THE RAPE in January of 1989," says Bill
Olson, sitting behind his desk in his law office in Grinnell.
"I had represented Steve and Nancy in various matters for four
or five years, and the woman who sat there that day . . . I had
not ever seen Nancy like that before. She was in very bad
shape, she looked as if somebody had really kicked her around
emotionally. They owed that money to the hospital, Mercy, as
I recall, and maybe a doctor or two, and they were looking for
some way that they could recover from somebody some way to
pay the bill. And they said, 'We thought if we just told you
what happened, you might be able to help us.' And then she
said, 'I was raped.'

"I asked her to tell me what happened, and I turned on my
tape recorder. She told me about getting to the lot at Grand
View, and she told me about the guy pushing his way into the
car, and then, she simply stopped. She just stopped. As ani-
mated as Nancy usually is, this time she had nothing to say.
She couldn't say it.

"I felt awful for her, and for the situation. She gets hurt and
what does she get out of it? Bills. I don't fault the hospital—as
I understood it, she had a supportive woman physician, and
Dee Ann, and Ralph Roth, who had become a hero to her. So
in that sense, everything went well—but now, here comes the
bill.

"So I told her I'd call Ralph and get some information, and see what we could do. What I was thinking about was a premises liability action against the college. I knew these things were iffy, but I thought it was worth investigating. My hope was that I could color fairly a cause of action, and make a monetary demand on Grand View. I wrote to the college, putting them on notice that I felt they might be liable, and that we'd be in touch with them. All I really wanted to do was get enough money for Steve and Nancy to pay their bills.

"Over the following months, with the help of the Des Moines Police Department, we began to put together crime statistics from the general neighborhood where Grand View is located. As we went along, I watched as Nancy began to inform herself, educating herself about the premises liability matter almost as intensely as she was doing with the criminal case.

"It became a self-starting thing for her. From time to time she would come by, when she felt Nan Horvat maybe wasn't telling her everything, or taking enough time with her, or when her own research would yield a term or an issue that was just Greek to her. She'd drop by here and leave a note: 'In the next couple of days I'd like to know what such-and-such means.' And so I'd copy something from the encyclopedia and highlight it, and put some notes on it, and off she'd go, back to the Grinnell College library.

"She needed to do this herself. She didn't need information supplied for her. It was part of her experience, to come to grips with it. I felt kind of useless during that early time, because I didn't know what to say. It was like dealing with The Widow, you know? What *do* you say? Pious, stupid things. So I pretty much kept my mouth shut, unless she asked me a question that I could help answer. And then I sort of felt useful.

"She wanted to *know*, she didn't want to have things just happen to her, or with respect to her, that she didn't understand. She wanted to take control. And that take-control thing became stronger as all the legal proceedings became more convoluted and protracted. She felt strongly that she ought to have some say in how the process went. She started expressing a lot of frustration and anger that, despite the fact that she was the victim, she was 'only a witness,' and not really party to the process. And she would refer to Nan as 'her lawyer' and I would say, kiddo, if you've got a lawyer, it's probably me.

"See, Nancy's always owed me money. A little here, a little there. But I've never hassled her on that, and she's always worked on paying me. She's been perfectly free to drop twenty-five bucks off whenever she wanted. I still believe that's why she trusts me.

"Anyway, I tried to explain Nan Horvat's role to her: that as prosecutor, she was concerned not just with Nancy but with all potential victims of Bobby Lee Smith. And that there were two rape cases she was prosecuting for the state at that point, which we all sometimes tended to forget. There was the other young woman, the one from Indianola. Two capital cases, essentially both at the same time. And with the DNA, there were some complex evidentiary details being dealt with here.

"I don't worship our system, but I just haven't seen a really good alternative to it that the American people could handle. Anthropologically, we're all so steeped in trial by jury, and all the safeguards of the Bill of Rights, and the adversary system.

"So anyway, it was kind of like, 'I am not going to be in a situation where I don't know what's happening around me.' Nancy's always had energy, she's never been passive. But this was different somehow. The beginning of an activist? I'm not sure that's what I was seeing at that point. I think an activist believes he or she is handling an issue on behalf of the public. For Nancy, all of this was still intensely personal, introspective, it was 'somebody's doing things that are having an impact on me.' She was not, for instance, thinking of other victims, not then. She was simply someone who was beginning to tackle a problem in a different way than she'd ever tackled her problems before."

•

A week before the scheduled trial date of March 15, I had a call from Nan Horvat. John Wellman had to withdraw from defending the case, she said. Bobby Lee Smith had been assigned new defense counsel, a man named Roger Owens. Because Owens was unfamiliar with the case, he would need additional time to prepare a defense. Essentially, he would have to start all over again. So the judge had granted the defense a continuance until June 7.

It would not be an exaggeration to say that I screamed. I screamed at Nan over the phone, I screamed at the walls of my house, and I screamed at anybody who got in my way over the next couple of days.

"What the *hell* happened?"

It turns out that Bobby Lee Smith, while he was sitting in the Polk County Jail, made a new friend. The guy's name was Charles Watkins, and he'd also been arrested for rape. As a matter of fact, one of Ralph Roth's cases. The rape that Watkins had been arrested for had happened on Court Avenue in Des Moines, within a few days of the two rapes that Bobby had been arrested for. Like Bobby, Charlie Watkins couldn't afford his own lawyer, so he was represented by the public defender's office—John Wellman.

The two men had evidently had one of those conversations that, if they'd been in a singles' bar, would've started out something like, "Do you come here often?" In their case, it was, "What are you in for?" Kidnapping and rape, says one. Kidnapping and rape, says the other. At which point, they individually contact John Wellman and each points the finger at the other. Watkins did it, says Smith. Smith did it, says Watkins. Bang! Big conflict of interest for Mr. Wellman.

Both men end up with new attorneys, and I end up with three months' hang time, and another in the long series of gentle lectures from Nan Horvat and Bill Olson about our wonderful constitutional system and the concept of the defendant's presumed innocence. It did not go down well.

•

One day, Benjamin didn't come home from kindergarten. During the week I always kept one eye on Sissy and my day-care kids and one eye on the clock, waiting for Nick and Ben to get home from school. Ben only had two blocks to walk after the bus dropped him off, and I had the trip timed right down to the minute. This day the minutes quickly piled up. He didn't walk in the door, and he didn't walk in the door, and he didn't—and I just knew. Somebody had snatched him, just as the rapist had promised.

I called Cathy Burnham and asked in panic if she'd come and watch the other kids for me, I had to go look for Ben. When she came through the door, I ran out, leaving a wailing Sissy behind, and got into the car, first driving the route he would've walked, then retracing all the way back to school. Nothing.

When I called Steven at work, he tried to get me to calm down. "Backtrack, Nancy," he said. "Call the school and start there."

They checked and told me Ben had boarded the bus when he was supposed to, but they'd be happy to radio the driver and find out where he'd ended up.

It turned out that he was giggling and goofing around with his friends on the bus, and so he'd gone right past his stop. In the time it took to find this out and get him back to where he was supposed to be, I had frightened Cathy, frightened Sissy, frightened Steven, galvanized the inner workings of the school system, and pictured every grisly detail of my son's kidnapping and death. I couldn't decide, once Ben was safely in the house, whether to whack his butt or hug the breath out of him. I felt the same when Nick walked in, just on general principles.

Sleep didn't come easy to us that night. "I just want a routine," I said to Steven. "I want us to be normal!" I wanted to take some things on faith, like the comings and goings of my kids on a school day. In fact, I wanted more

than anything to be bored by the predictability of my life
with my family. But no matter what we did or how hard we
tried, being normal seemed farther and farther out of reach.
And the only thing even close to boring was waiting for it all
to be over.

CHAPTER TEN

ONE NIGHT IN LATE MARCH, I was at the high school gym with Cathy and Keith Burnham, watching all our children perform for their Sports Club event. It was half-time of the high school basketball game, and the kids were doing all kinds of skill and coordination activities—gymnastics, tumbling, jumping rope.

When the Sports Club presentation was over and the basketball game headed into the second half, Cathy said she didn't really feel like hanging around for the rest of the game. I suggested that the two of us leave, taking my car, and Keith could watch the end of the game and bring the kids home in his car. When she said that was fine with her, we cleared the plan with Keith, and left the gym.

Cathy and I walked out to the parking lot, with me of course jumping at shadows every step of the way. We could see our breath in the air, it was so cold. Once we'd settled in the car, she suddenly turned to me and said, "Nancy, I really need to tell you something."

Her voice sounded so strained, and I thought, Oh, God, somebody's sick. Or she's leaving him. Or he's leaving her. I immediately felt guilty—I'd done nothing for weeks except rant and rave about my own problems, the damn court case, the damn continuance. I started the car to get the heater going and then I turned toward her, bracing myself for the news.

"I was raped," she said.

"*What?*" I gasped. "What? When?"

"When I was nineteen," she said. She was thirty-two now.

It was back when she and Keith had been dating, she said. They'd been at a bar, and she'd left ahead of him. That was where the guy grabbed her.

She had never reported it, never gotten counseling, never told anyone but Keith. And she could remember every detail as though it had happened the day before.

"For years," she said, "I've had these nightmares. Oh, not specifically that night or his face. But about being chased. I run and run, trying to get away from someone, but I never can. He gets me. And I always wake up before I find out who it is."

I was dumbfounded. I knew, because I was collecting them in my notebooks, most of the recent statistics on rape: It will eventually touch one out of every three women; in the United States, rape occurs once every six minutes of every single day; only one woman in ten will ever report the attack. And because so few victims can bring themselves to report a sexual assault, these estimates are viewed as low. I was getting to know these numbers almost as well as I knew my children's birthdays, yet here I was, sitting in the car, astonished that somebody I knew had actually been raped.

"You have to follow this case through, Nancy," Cathy said. "No matter what. Please. You have to stick with it, you have to go to court, you have to nail this guy. For all of us."

It wasn't the first time I'd heard the inclusive "us" used by a victim—we all said it in the group counseling sessions. But this was my neighbor, my friend. I had always believed that she lived in that "other" world, the safe one I tried to retreat to when all this "rape stuff," as I called it, threatened to overwhelm me. But Cathy's "us" was too close to home—now there was a recognizable face on the big, muddy mass of statistics. I knew now that when I looked in the mirror, it wouldn't be just my own face looking back at me.

Cathy had been living with the memory and her nightmares for thirteen years; who knows how much longer she might have kept dragging the bad dreams around with her? As I tried to comfort her I wondered, Who else did I not know about? Who else among my friends and relatives had been keeping secrets like this? I felt suddenly helpless at the recognition that *every single one* of those numbers I'd collected so carefully was somebody's friend, or sister, or daughter, or mother, or wife. Real women, like Cathy and me, held like hostages in what was beginning to look and feel more and more like an epidemic.

In April, the news about the horrible rape and beating of a woman jogger in New York's Central Park hit the newspapers and the television news.

It was as if I had developed some kind of weird antennae—every time I saw a headline like this, I had to drop whatever I was doing and pay attention in a new kind of intense way. Had this stuff been happening all along and I'd just ignored it? Ignored it because it happened in a city, or because it happened to somebody I didn't know? Because it didn't seem to have anything to do with me?

The jogger had been beaten unconscious, and left in the park to die. She still might die. At the very least, they said, she would probably be left with some brain damage. And there would be DNA testing, because she probably wouldn't be able to identify anyone. It seemed like an awfully big price to pay for simply taking a run around a park. . . . I thought about the students from Grinnell College who run near campus all the time. It could've been one of them.

The jogger had evidently been attacked by a whole gang of teenagers. She'd been running at night, the news said. Why was she there at night, I asked, and knew almost as soon as the question had formed in my head that it was another one of "those" questions. The question that should've come first was: Why did someone hurt her?

And all the commentators were talking about the race of the kids who'd been accused. They were black. She was white. They're talking about this in the wrong way, I mumbled to myself, unable to stop listening to all the talking heads. This isn't about race, about what whites and blacks do to each other. It's about a bunch of men trying to kill one woman. Holding her down, beating her, stealing her life. Hang in there, jogger, I prayed. I didn't know her name.

On Memorial Day weekend, 1989, the court granted Bobby Lee Smith and his attorneys another continuance on the trial date, moving it from June 7 to August 14.

It was the DNA evidence that was causing the problem, Nan Horvat tried to explain to me. Our side (I was still using the possessive) had provided the defense lawyer, Roger Owens, with everything he'd requested: all the medical records from the hospital, all the legal records from Ralph Roth's office, and everything we had from the FBI about the laboratory work they'd done on the DNA. But the defense was overwhelmed, and out of money to have its own set of tests done, and besides, because John Wellman had to withdraw, Owens had to start all over again, and needed more time. So the court gave him what he wanted—more money, more time, and a second attorney, Cynthia Moisan, just to handle the part of the case that hinged on the DNA tests.

"But that means he's getting two attorneys, paid for with my tax dollars!" I protested. "Why can't I get one attorney specifically to represent me?"

Nan had her hands full. For one thing, she was prosecuting the other rape that Smith was accused of, as well as mine. Why couldn't the court accommodate *me* for once, with extra lawyers and extra money? Nan's calm response: "You're just the witness in this case, Nancy. You don't need an attorney."

I called Bill Olson in a fury. I needed another attorney to tell me that what was happening was legitimate, that this was the way the system was supposed to work.

"Maybe not," Bill told me, "but this is the way it is."

"But why?" I bitched to anyone who would listen. Why is it our side that has to bend and bend, and their side that gets more and more concessions?

"They're not getting all that many concessions, Nancy," Bill said. "Nan is prosecuting the two cases here, and Owens is defending them both. Everybody's got a full plate. Try to be patient while the process works."

Process! I'd always thought process was when you moved forward. This didn't feel like process to me, it felt like trying to run in a dream, and knowing you're not moving.

Then summer came, and the children were home from school for vacation. Ben and Sissy had birthdays. And it got hot. My God, it got hot. It was the drought of 1989, and everything as far as I could see was dry and brown and next to dead. The heat lightning would crack in the sky at night, and the thunder would roll, but the rain wouldn't come. I used to enjoy puttering in my yard, but not now. Everything wilted, it seemed, within minutes of going into the ground. There was no relief anywhere.

CHAPTER ELEVEN

THIS IS ONE OF THE BEST JOBS a lawyer could ever have," says Nan Horvat, assistant prosecutor for Polk County. "That's not to demean people who defend criminal cases, because I think they're some of the best attorneys in the world. They have to take cases that are unpopular and make sure those defendants have their rights protected. I have great respect for the public defender, John Wellman, who terrorizes me regularly. And I have equal respect for Roger Owens. But in what I do, I deal with people who have been maimed or robbed or violated in some way, and I'm in the position to help them. So I think it's a great job.

"Nancy Ziegenmeyer was unusual, different from most victims. Quite frankly, I think that if I were a victim of a crime, I'd probably behave like Nancy did. She wanted to know what was going on.

"I gave her my office number and my home number. She never called me at home, I don't think, but she did call the office a lot with questions. Most victims, when I'm working with them on a case, don't call, ever, and I worry about them. But Nancy would get upset with me over the phone, and that's normal. Often, I have to explain complicated legal things over the phone, and it's not a good medium for that.

"The law sets out very specific goals for us as prosecutors. After a person is arrested, I have forty-five days to formally charge him with the crime and file the trial information. From that period I have ninety days, and he has the right to be tried within that period. Bobby Lee Smith waived that ninety-day period. Because of whatever legal reasons he and his counsel had, he agreed to go beyond that. Sometimes defendants don't waive that right, and you can't blame them. They're sitting in jail, the jail's not air-conditioned, it's very unpleasant—it's much easier to do your time in prison, where you can move around, go to the weight room, go to the library.

"When John Wellman had to withdraw as Smith's defense attorney, and Roger Owens and Cindy Moisan were appointed, they had to start over again, from scratch, to build their own case. That's just good law. The FBI had done their work on the DNA, and Roger and Cindy wanted to have the same opportunity for another lab, an independent lab, to run the same tests. That can be done, if there's enough of a sample left, and there was in this case. So it was good law, and it was good science. DNA was still new enough in criminal prosecutions—and somewhat controversial—that I wanted to do it right. And obviously the defense did, too. I didn't want 'doing it wrong' to show up later in an appeal.

"By law, I'm required to give the defense notice of all the witnesses and some general sense of what they will say. All the DNA evidence that was part of our case had to go to the defense, and when both sides cooperate in this manner, it can sometimes look to crime victims as though the prosecutor and the defense are collaborating, not being adversarial the way people expect, and the way victims want. People really want that 'us versus them' stuff. Hey, I watch all the TV shows about lawyers and trials—they're fun, and sometimes maybe even a little educational. But they give a slightly tilted idea about how we really go about our business.

"Roger's a great lawyer, and he represents his clients zealously in court, and he means to do a good job. So do I. In court, it would appear that we try to out-yell each other, or one of us might want to be more . . . well, emphatic than the other one. But when we leave the courtroom, I don't battle with him. He's doing his job, I'm doing mine. And my job, as the prosecution, was to produce what the defense requested, and the defense requested a lot of information from the FBI.

"So Roger would file a motion for the prosecution to produce their evidence, and then I would request whatever it was from the FBI—access to their records, their testing procedures, their lab. And since Nancy Ziegenmeyer's case was one of the first rape cases the FBI ever had to handle (up until then, they'd used the science mainly for forensics), they didn't anticipate all our production requests. Some people might say they took their time. Other people might say they deliberately balked. Maybe they thought those pesky lawyers out there in Iowa would eventually just give up and go away.

"Nancy was very frustrated that, as a victim, she didn't have more direct involvement in the actual trial preparation. You can understand that if you were hit by a car, for instance, and there was a civil suit, you'd have a lot more involvement. You'd be sitting there with your lawyer, and maybe your insurance company. In a case like that, you're the injured party. In criminal cases, you're just not given the same level of participation because, quite literally, you're *not* the injured party. The State's the injured party. And you are the witness to that injury.

"This always comes as a surprise to people who haven't been through the system. In the prosecutor's office, we have a policy: We always check both with the police and the victims before we do things, to keep everybody posted on what's going on, to try and eliminate these surprises. But the first time through . . . well, it's tough.

"And there's a popular perception, again from TV, maybe, of the overloaded prosecutor, and that the reason a victim feels pushed aside is because I'm juggling too many cases. That's probably true in some cities, but it's not true here. If I'm overloaded, it's because I self-impose it. I pay great attention to every detail when I'm prosecuting a case, because I want to make sure I do it right. I want to win. But not being able to give Nancy what she needed and wanted was never because I was overwhelmed with my caseload. After all, this isn't New York or Los Angeles.

"I understood why Nancy's anger grew, but I also knew I had a very specific job to do. I'm very strong, and I don't like being bossed around. Neither does Nancy. She likes to talk, to argue. So do I—that's why I became a lawyer. So the way we worked it out was, first I'd boss for a while, then she'd boss for a while, then I'd boss for a while. We took turns bossing."

"If we're going to put people away, deprive them of their liberty, then we better do it right," says Roger Owens, former Polk County public defender. "Good prosecutors, and this is to Nan Horvat's credit, will give you everything in their file, because once we convict people . . . I mean, if we're going to convict them, we ought to do it by the rules. A lot of prosecutors have the idea that, 'I'm going to withhold this, and then I'll do that, and then I'll fake 'em out over there,' just to get a conviction. But Nan's the best they've got, she takes a case and works it straight.

"The general public believes that the defendants have more rights than the police. Until you're caught in the system, and then you find out that's bullshit. Being the defendant these days means you have the right to have a lawyer before you're hung. Little by little, we've whittled away at the Fourth Amendment, the Sixth Amendment, the Fourteenth Amendment. And once those rights get taken away, nobody comes along and puts them back. And then once every ten years or so, the Supreme Court will say, 'This mass murderer's rights were violated!' Imagine how blatant that violation had to be in order to get somebody's attention!

"People don't understand the system until they're in it, including the defendants. Maybe it's because we're not teaching civics. Oh, we're teaching our kids about money, and how to balance a checkbook, and God forbid we don't teach them how to keep up with Japan. But we're not giving them what they need to understand the role that the Bill of Rights plays in this justice system.

"I ask prospective jurors if they can extend the same presumption of innocence to that guy at the table that they'd extend if he was their kid, or their brother, and they look at me like I must be joking. 'It's never going to happen to me,' they think, 'it's never going to be my son or daughter sitting there.' But when it does happen to you, or your kid, watch the fireworks!

"For instance, in this state, we set a mandatory jail sentence for possession of over an ounce of marijuana. Five years. Until some big muckamuck's kid got picked up, and I'll be goddamned if that law wasn't changed in a month. See? Because it's never going to happen to anyone *we* know.

"I knew early on we were looking at a DNA analysis in this case, and that's when I brought in Cynthia Moisan, who had previously worked on DNA cases and is really up on the science. In fact, Cindy and Nan probably know more about DNA than the FBI—that is, if anybody really knows anything about DNA. I'm a halfway educated man and I don't understand it, and I think anyone who tells me they really understand it is just flat out lying. What we've done here is, we've created another branch of the government, just for statistics

"And we've got this rape shield law now, which I disagree with wholeheartedly, because it just denies people fair trials—I can't even go into someone's history of lying. Say a woman's accused five other people before, I can't even ask about that. Doesn't seem right.

"Another thing about this trial was, instead of the continuances dragging on one at a time, month to month, early on we should've said, hey, look, we're having all this hassle with the DNA and the FBI, why don't we just set the damn thing for six months from now. In June, we should've set it for November. Then whatever happened before we got to trial could've happened each time without setting everybody up for the frustration. Nancy kept getting ready, then being let down, Bobby kept getting ready, then being let down. It was hard on everybody.

"I guess we weren't very sensitive to Nancy. As part of the system, my job is to represent the defendant. But having said that, it doesn't mean damn everyone else.

"On the other hand, that frustration doesn't have anything to do with the Bill of Rights. It doesn't say in the Bill of Rights, let's hang the son of a bitch so the victim can get on with her life.

"On the *other* hand, I've got two daughters. And I do think rape is a national problem. But I think people accused of it are entitled to the protection of the Constitution.

"It gets to you sometimes, the whole thing. I was chief public defender here for ten years, and then I just burned out. I was home one day, at the dinner table, and said, 'Pass the fucking salt.' My wife looked at me and said, 'You know, Roger, it's about time you think about leaving this job.' "

CHAPTER TWELVE

IN JULY, ANOTHER SETBACK. Nan had gone back into court to make an argument that there should be one big trial, incorporating all the elements in the case. She asked that the charges in my case, the charges in the Indianola woman's case, and the theft charges against Lisa Davis (whom Ralph had arrested as an accessory, because of my rings) all be heard at one time.

The court said no, and scheduled the three cases out over the calendar. The Indianola woman's case would begin on August 23, the theft trial against Lisa Davis would be heard September 13, and "my" case got continued again, from August 14 to September 15.

The word *continuance* rang in my ear like every obscenity I'd ever heard. "Why is this happening?" I railed to Nan day after day on the phone. "Why do I have to keep *my* life on hold? Why do I have to put up with this shit?" I pictured her holding the phone out from her ear at least six inches. I was sure everyone else in her office could hear. I didn't care.

Her voice was almost always calm when she replied, which enraged me even further. She reminded me of every reasonable schoolteacher I'd ever had.

"Nancy, there's one good thing about this. If we can get Bobby Lee Smith convicted on the Indianola woman's charges, he'll get the maximum, a life sentence, with no parole. And then we won't have to go to court on your case."

Did I hear that right? Not go to court? Not go in there, after all this time—nearly a year of weepy days and endless nights of bad dreams and claustrophobia, and wandering from room to room, counting my children to make sure they were all still there, and locking and relocking doors—not go in there, after all this hell, and point my finger and shout, "He did it!"?

"How could you think for one minute," I demanded, "that my not going to court would be a good thing?"

The Constitution guaranteed Bobby Lee Smith a fair trial. Well, I told Nan, I wanted *my* fair trial. I wanted my day in court, goddamnit, I wanted it more than I had ever wanted anything in my life, and I wanted it now. The defendant's right to face his accuser never meant more to me. Face me, you bastard, I thought. Face me.

For a man who rarely expresses an opinion, my husband is the most opinionated man I've ever known. Steven is quiet, and I'm noisy, so it's easy sometimes for people to forget that he's in the room. But he's there, and he's paying attention, and he's keeping score. He waits, and watches, and withholds judgment until he's good and ready. "Calm down," he'd been telling me all this time, "you're getting the kids in an uproar." But underneath it, he was as angry and frustrated as I was. He watched while our lives kept getting put on hold, and now, he'd finally reached the limit of his patience.

Sometime during the summer, he had clipped an editorial from the *Des Moines Register*, written by the *Register*'s editor, Geneva Overholser. Now he brought it to me, saying, "Read this. Maybe you should think about doing something like this."

The column, titled "American Shame: The Stigma of Rape" read as follows:

> I understand why newspapers tend not to use rape vic-
> tims' names. No crime is more horribly invasive, more

brutally intimate. In no crime does the victim risk being blamed, and in so insidious a way: She asked for it, she wanted it. Perhaps worst of all, there's the judgment: She's damaged goods, less desirable, less marriageable.

This stigma, this enormously unfair onus, brought most newspaper editors years ago to conclude that they shouldn't worsen the plight of rape victims by naming them in the newspaper. Why violate a rape victim twice, feminists asked editors. With rape victims refusing to testify in court for fear of exposure to the public glare, that has been a compelling argument.

As feminist and editor, I respect and respond to these arguments. Indeed, the policy of the Des Moines Register is generally not to use the name of rape victims. Yet I surely wish it could be otherwise.

It's not the law that keeps journalists from using rape victims' names. The Supreme Court in late June overturned the conviction of a Florida weekly newspaper for violating state law by publishing the name of a rape victim.

Yet the decision is unlikely to change the fact that no more than 5 to 10 percent of newspapers routinely use rape victims' names. It is, as the New York Times said, "one of modern journalism's few conspiracies of silence."

A tenet of journalism holds that we ought to come as close as possible to printing the facts as we know them. Going against this rule in the case of rape victims feels to me very much like participating in the onus, the stigma, that I find so unjust. Editors do not hesitate to name the victim of a murder attempt. Does not our very delicacy in dealing with rape victims subscribe to the idea that rape is a crime of sex rather than the crime of brutal violence that it really is?

Surely the sour blight of prejudice is best subjected to strong sunlight. Take homosexuality: Until recently, very few gay men or lesbians sought public identification.

Now, many identify themselves assertively and proudly. Newspaper treatment of gay issues has evolved apace. And society's understanding of homosexuality has grown and matured.

Or take AIDS. New Yorkers' awareness of the cruelty of AIDS is far ahead of that of many parts of the country. Sheer numbers are a primary reason. How many New Yorkers know someone who has died of AIDS? How many have read of a prominent and respected figure, a vital contributor to society, who has? The simple fact of listing AIDS-related deaths helps public awareness grow.

Yet, across the country, newspapers still struggle with whether to list AIDS as a cause of death, and even with how to get the information—because loved ones, and health officials, resist, believing the information will reflect negatively on the deceased. The onus is the victor, public understanding the loser.

And think of abortion. For years, few women would admit to having had an abortion. Then prominent women and, gradually, growing numbers of women from all walks of life began to step forward and tell their stories. And, accordingly, public awareness grew.

These days the public testimony of courageous rape victims like Susan Estrich, Michael Dukakis's presidential campaign manager, or actress Kelly McGillis is beginning to have the same effect.

But that public witness was Estrich's choice. It is not for the newspaper editor, eyes fixed on distant virtue, to sacrifice today's unwilling victims. If I seek a world in which newspapers routinely print rape victims' names, it is also a world in which rape victims are treated compassionately, the stigma eradicated.

So I am unwilling to sacrifice today's unwilling victims for long-term good. Yet I believe that we will not break down the stigma until more and more women take public stands. I will go on with the general rule, as most newspapers do, despite my dislike of it.

But I urge women who have suffered this awful crime and attendant injustice to speak out, as a few are beginning to do, and identify themselves.

Rape is an American shame. Our society needs to see that and attend to it, not hide it or hush it up. As long as rape is deemed unspeakable—and is therefore not fully and honestly spoken of—the public outrage will be muted as well.

I had to read the editorial two or three times before everything in it began to sink into my brain. To speak out? To point my own finger at myself? To stand in front of my neighbors, my town? My whole state? How would I go about doing such a thing? For three weeks, Steven and I talked about what this decision might mean for us.

We already knew about what Overholser called the "rape stigma"—the raised eyebrows, the stupid questions. Where were you, what time of night was it, why were you in that part of town, what were you wearing, did you fight, did you know him? And we understood that ultimately, none of those questions mattered. What mattered was consent. Or the lack of it. I had not given my consent to my rapist. But to give my consent to a newspaper. . . .

Rape wasn't just what happened at that very moment, it was everything that came afterward, and it just seemed to drag on forever. I had believed that what I needed was justice, some satisfaction for my loss, and I had believed that justice would come from "my" system. But it turned out, of course, that the system I thought was mine was also Bobby Lee Smith's. Because of that, it looked as if justice was going to take its own sweet time. And I was hardly happy—or productive— mumbling "To hell with the Constitution" under my breath.

There had to be another way, a way to make people pay attention. A way to make an impact, to make a change. And maybe even a way to get help for others. I knew I was way ahead of some rape survivors: I had Steven, I had the kids, I had my mom. I had people like Dee Ann and Ralph on my side, and Nan with her endless, infuriating integrity, and Cathy with her faith, and Penny who always acted like nothing had changed, and Diane and Ron, and Gramma and Grampa. I had people who knew, and helped, and comforted me. And I also knew—I'd always known this—that I was a fighter, and that I'd keep fighting no matter how many continuances they threw at me. But what about all the others?

I called the *Des Moines Register* and asked to speak to Geneva Overholser.

I'd never picked up a telephone and called a newspaper editor before. I'd never even written a letter to an editor. I sat there with the phone in my hand, listening to it ring, wondering if I'd finally gone around the bend. Would this Overholser woman think I was some kind of nut case?

I was surprised, and relieved, to find that I didn't have to go through three receptionists and four secretaries before getting to her. I first spoke with Lorraine Keller, her assistant, and told her I was calling about the editorial about rape. Lorraine was nice—so far, so good, I thought.

When Geneva came to the phone, I blurted out who I was, what had happened to me, what I'd been thinking. I told her I was angry, that I'd done everything I was supposed to, but it didn't seem to be working. She said she was willing to listen. We made an appointment for me to go to Des Moines, to meet with her and talk further.

"This decision is completely yours to make," Steven told me. If I did it, if I didn't do it, either way, he'd support me. We went over and over the ramifications of what it would mean for us, our family, our already fragile sense of safety. Of privacy.

"If this is what it will take for you to get control of your life back," he said, "then I'll do whatever I can to support you."

Within days, Steven and I had been to Des Moines, talked to Geneva Overholser, and had a *Register* reporter, Jane Schorer, assigned to the story. My God, I thought. We're actually going to do this.

At that first meeting, Geneva quizzed us both about what it might mean to go public with our story. She didn't talk down to us, but it was clear she knew more about what we were getting into than we did, and she wanted to make sure we were prepared. Once the decision had been made, we went home, confident that telling the story was the right thing to do.

Then the second thoughts started to sneak in. I was terrified that we'd inadvertently do something to jeopardize the trial outcome. And Nan was mad when I told her about the story— she thought they were going to print it now. No, I promised her, Geneva and Jane assured me that there would be nothing printed until the trial was over and a verdict announced (and who knew, I shrugged, when the hell that will be). In the meantime, Jane would get to know me, and Steven. She'd come to Grinnell, and talk to the police, and the lawyers, and she'd follow the case until it ended with a verdict. The *Register* had also assigned a photographer, David Peterson. He'd won a Pulitzer Prize two years before for his pictures of the farm crisis.

The idea of pictures alerted us to the need to set up a few ground rules. Our house, our home, had to be off limits. No Jane in the house, no David, no pictures of the house itself. No interviews with or pictures of the children. We had to keep one place private, one sanctuary, for the kids, and for ourselves. Everybody agreed.

Once all the wheels had been set in motion, we knew we had no choice but to trust Jane and David. But we also knew there were some hard questions we'd better ask ourselves before we went any further.

"Are we going to tell them the truth?" I asked Steven.

"Which part?" he asked, knowing very well which part.

The part about us not being married anymore. The part about the divorce in 1988, when I ran away and left him. The part about the reconciliation that had happened just weeks before the rape in the parking lot. The part about all the mistakes we'd made, and paid for.

As always, Steven thought before he spoke, and when the words came out, they were clear and precise. "We don't want any surprises coming up in court. We don't want those lawyers throwing anything at you that isn't relevant. So we'll tell the truth, to Jane Schorer and anybody else who asks."

But could I really do that, I wondered?

"Let it all come out," he said. "You were raped, Nancy, and that bastard's going to pay for it. If anybody thinks he can prove to me or anybody else that what we went through before has a goddamned thing to do with the hell we're going through now, I'd sure like to see him try."

CHAPTER THIRTEEN

STEVEN AND I WERE MARRIED in June 1981. Our wedding was held in the front yard of the little farmhouse we'd rented a few miles outside of Grinnell, on a gentle rise surrounded by cornfields. There was an old tree, with a tire swing, and a big, wonderful kitchen. Our friends came, and our families, and we had kegs of icy beer, and a beautiful cake iced with yellow flowers with green leaves, baked by my brand-new mother-in-law. The music we'd taped for the wedding was playing inside the house, and during the ceremony we could hear it through the open windows. The sun was shining, and the sky was blue, and there was a slight breeze blowing. Steven wore a white tux, and he just seemed to grin all day. The bride was blooming—after all, she was three months pregnant, with more bosom than she'd ever had before in her whole life, and long hair, way down past her shoulders, and a big grin of her own. It was a perfect day.

Not far from that farmhouse was the big white house where my great-grandmother had lived when I was a little girl. I can close my eyes right now and tell you where every piece of furniture was in that house. When we would go to visit her there, she would have baked fresh cookies for us. We'd run to the kitchen and steal the homemade noodles off her chopping board, and then she'd pretend to go after our little fingers with a knife, and we'd hoot and holler, and run away, and then she'd laugh.

What she gave us, and what my grandparents had given me, was the kind of life I believed I wanted for Steven and me and our kids: a safe, happy life, with laughter and the smells of cooking, in a big old house of our own. I had never wanted a new house, with all the modern things, like all my girlfriends did. I had dreamed of an old one, that I could work on and restore. I would raise my kids in it, and Steven and I would grow old in it, and that would be all I'd ever need. And I really believed, on that June morning, as Steven and I stood out there under the trees and married each other, that I was on my way to that dream. I had just turned twenty.

Within thirty-six months, I'd had three children, and the dream had grown a little raggedy. When well-meaning people ask me why we had our kids so fast, I have only one answer: because we wanted them fast. But now I was tired, and Steven was tired, and we were wondering just how we'd gotten where we were. We started to fight. We fought about little things, we fought about big things. One of the babies was usually crying, and sometimes all three would cry at once.

It had all happened so fast since that first day, and now we suddenly found ourselves—or rather, I found myself, because Steven had always been there—in grown-up land. Some days I just wanted to be Grampa's little girl again and go shopping for a new dress, except now I had a little girl of my own, and new dresses were luxuries. Steven was working hard, six days a week, but we were stretching his salary thin as cheesecloth. So I went to work, waitressing and tending bar.

We juggled the kids from place to place, between Steven's mother's house and my mother's house. In between, we'd have an occasional paid baby-sitter, but they were hard to afford. Steven worked days and I'd usually work nights. Time together was scarce.

We bought our own house in Grinnell after Sissy was born, when Nicholas was almost two and Benjamin was thirteen months old. That was the first time Bill Olson did any legal work for us—he prepared the documents for the real estate closing. I wasn't happy about leaving the little farmhouse and moving into town, but the demands of two job schedules and the three babies made it impractical to be so far away from things like grocery stores, pediatricians, and baby-sitters. And one day soon, of course, the kids would be going to school.

A strange thing had happened a year or so before the move. Not long after Nick was born, a social worker from the Department of Human Services contacted me. She'd had a report, she said, and needed to take a close look at the baby.

I was appalled, and a little frightened. I'd made a couple of mistakes—what new mother doesn't?—but I sure didn't think I'd ever done anything that would bring the Department of Human Services after me. Who on earth, I asked her, had filed this report? She said she wasn't allowed to reveal that information.

Scared, I stood and watched as the social worker carefully examined my little boy. Two weeks later, the report came back marked "Unfounded" and we heard nothing else. Steven and I were both unnerved, but we didn't have much faith in bureaucracies, so we figured it was just some kind of error on their part.

Then, when Ben was a baby, the Department of Human Services sent another social worker. They'd had a second report, they said. This time, the complaint was that I was repeatedly kicking and beating Ben, possibly damaging his kidneys. I couldn't believe this was happening again. Who is saying these things, I demanded. They couldn't tell me, they said. It was confidential.

Once again, nervous and scared, I let another one of my boys be examined, because what would happen, I thought, if I didn't do what they said? They'd think I was guilty of something for sure. And once again, a couple of weeks later, the report came back marked "Unfounded."

But by the time it happened a third time, when Sissy was a baby, I was prepared. Grinnell is a small town, with a grapevine that works better than AT&T, and now both Steven and

I were pretty sure we knew who had been complaining about the kind of mother I was.

I was in the kitchen that day with all three kids, and we were making a lot of noise and a big mess with the mixer and a bowl full of cookie dough. The phone rang, and it was another social worker, telling me she was on her way over. Another anonymous report of child abuse had been filed. I said oh, fine, why don't you just get a court order before you come to my house this time! And then I called Bill Olson and told him what had been going on.

Once again, after an examination of Sissy that managed to scare her and the little boys, the official report from Human Services came back marked "Unfounded." We'd had just about enough.

In November 1986, Bill Olson had a restraining order issued for Wilma Ziegenmeyer, preventing her from seeing or interfering with or contacting the children without express consent from me and Steven. He also requested a complete copy of all the reports from the Iowa Department of Human Services. When they sent the material to him, the name and all references to "the informant" had been deleted, but the chronology and the details—the who-said-what-to-whom—told the whole story. Steven and I and Bill Olson didn't have to be a trio of detectives to know that what we'd guessed (and heard, on the trusty town grapevine) was true. Wilma had done it.

She had told them I beat my kids repeatedly; she'd told them that the kids weren't fed, weren't cared for. She'd told them that Steven had a severe drinking problem that made him neglect the kids, and that they were often left to their own devices. When Steven and I confronted her, she denied the whole thing.

When the injunction was served on Wilma, she called Bill Olson's office, leaving messages with his secretary that I was a "paranoid schizophrenic" (she'd taken a couple of extension courses in psychology) and that "the blood of those children will be on your hands!" She then sent a twenty-seven-page handwritten letter to the Department of Social Services describing every move I'd made for three years. The gruesome details, however, were of her own strange imaginings.

There was no point in denying my temper—I had a bad one, and still do. There was no denying that Steven drank more beer than was good for him—he did, and still does. But my mother-in-law, who'd seen me as a curse on her life since day one, had reinvented us as monsters, and our children as victims. At one point, she'd even checked herself into a private Christian mental hospital, telling the doctors there that her daughter-in-law, the child abuser, had driven her crazy. And once charges like these are made—especially in a small town—they hang in the air like a black cloud, and all the "unfounded" reports and restraining orders in the world won't make them go away. Steven and I were already struggling with the reality of two strong personalities, three babies, and not enough money to go around. We didn't need this, too.

As the months passed, fighting was pretty much all we did. I hollered and yelled, Steven began to drink heavily, and wouldn't yell back, which made me even angrier. I stayed later and later at the bar on the nights I worked, drinking with my friends and dreading going home. On the nights I stayed at home and didn't work, Steven would drink steadily until he went up to bed drunk and mad, and he didn't have much to say to me in the meantime. Over time, the disintegration gathered a weight and a momentum all its own. Like a big rock rolling down a hill, it stood a good chance of smashing us flat.

In the winter of 1987/88, I went to Bill Olson. It's Steven's drinking, I told him. If I can just get him sober, we'll be OK. With Bill's help, I filed a complaint, and had Steven committed to the state hospital, Mt. Pleasant, for an alcohol rehabilitation program. What I did scared me, but I really believed I was doing the right thing.

After only three days, Steven came home, angry and resentful. Needless to say, what I'd done had been a simplistic solution to a complicated problem, and it changed nothing. In fact, it made everything worse. After a few more weeks, I went back to Bill, and filed for divorce.

And then I left my family and went to Oklahoma with another man.

There are few other details about that time in our lives, and my behavior during it, that are worth remembering or repeating now. I ran away, is what I did, not knowing at that point that when you run away, you take yourself and all your problems right along with you.

Steven stayed in our home, with the children, and told me I'd always have a home there, if I wanted it. He paid my bills. He accepted my collect telephone calls, and gave me advice on my relationship, which was a stupid one. He never dated, never saw other women. He sobered up and waited it out.

In September 1988, the divorce became final. A few weeks later, I came back home and asked Steven to take me back. I had actually been gone only five or six weeks.

Whatever it was that had happened to us, it was over. We tried to pick up our lives and start over again, never thinking for one minute that it would be easy or painless. We knew we had a lot of work to do, and I knew I had a lot to make up for. I started in the simplest way: I took my three children out trick-or-treating. And I didn't go back to work in the bar. With Steven's encouragement, I started studying for the real estate test. And on November 19, I was raped.

So that morning, when I ran into Mercy Hospital's emergency room in tears, it was with the sickening certainty that, this time, I'd surely pushed Steven too far. *This* he would not be able to forgive. *This* I had coming. In the long weeks and months before the trial started, when I asked God, "When can I say I've learned my lesson?" I was speaking from the heart of the rape victim's agony: I must've had it coming.

And when I decided to reveal my identity and the details of my rape, it was with the fear that it would make perfect sense to everybody. Most of Grinnell already knew how I'd behaved when Steven and I were having trouble. They knew about the divorce. And I'd already had plenty of days when I felt as if I was pushing my grocery cart around the Fairway market in my underwear. Now what would "they" think? Of course Nancy Ziegenmeyer was raped. She was a bad girl.

CHAPTER FOURTEEN

I WAS AT MT. PLEASANT about three days," says Steven Ziegenmeyer. He wears cowboy boots and jeans. He doesn't abide fools or pretentiousness, and only wears suits to funerals. He looks off somewhere in the distance before he speaks, and his sentences have long pauses between them. When the words come out, they frequently come out rough. "She was working one night, and I was fixing the kids supper, and then here she comes, with a couple of deputies, and hauled my ass to Mt. Pleasant that very night.

"Those people there, they get paid by the state, but I never ran into a one of them that had half an ounce of common sense. They wanted me to stay for one of those thirty-day-dry-you-out programs and I said, guys, forget this bullshit. I mean, I can't afford to do this, take a month off and play footsie with you people, it's not in my budget here. I'm not going to argue that I drink a hell of a lot more than I should, that's a fact. Everybody that knows me knows that; my best friends have climbed my ass for how much I drink for years and years, ever since I was in high school.

"The second day, maybe, was Friday. That was pay weekend, and I got paid on Friday. Nancy went and picked up my check, but she couldn't cash it. So she calls me at Mt. Pleasant and says if I bring your check, will you sign it? I said fuck you, you're the one that had me locked up in here, you figure out

NANCY ZIEGENMEYER · 97

how the hell to feed the family. She got me out, the next Tuesday. She said she'd done it because she loved me; she wanted to help me quit my drinking. But it just made me mad.

"Later on, in spring, she'd been working for Reg and Darlene Campbell, at the lounge, out by the Best Western. With what she was making with tips and stuff, she wanted a new car. I thought, well, maybe she's going to accept a little responsibility here. She didn't have any credit rating, so I put my name on the contract, and my name's the one on the payment book. That's when we got the little blue car, the GrandAm.

"But things stayed bad. I don't know when she met this guy from Oklahoma, or wherever. He was up here with a crew working on some power lines. I'd hear things from other people, but then I started reading it on my telephone bill.

"She told me she was going. I didn't really understand why, it didn't make good sense to me, other than maybe she was having an early midlife crisis or something. I don't know what it was. She was just running, running.

"She came out to the shop, where I work. She'd gotten the divorce papers, and wanted me to sign them, and to sign the ninety-day waiver, the waiver of counseling. I just said, oh, no, I don't think I will. And she screamed at me, and slammed the car door and roared off in a cloud of gravel. But there was no stopping her. Eventually I signed the damn papers.

"The original understanding was that she was going to go to Oklahoma and establish herself there, with a job, a house, some way to support the kids. In the meantime, she'd leave them with me, to finish the school year. When she came back to get them, Nick wouldn't go. The other two, Ben and Sissy, they wanted to go with their momma. They were just babies then. I let 'em go, but I didn't like it a goddamn bit. A while after that was when she came home.

"I covered all her expenses while she was gone. And I took care of the kids, and paid for the collect calls, and talked with her on the phone. And I listened. I figured that sooner or later, she'd find out that this goose wasn't the golden egg that maybe she thought he was. I just thought all right, I'll try to be nice with this, I'll try to wait it out.

"When she did come home, she said she'd been wrong. It was like she got religion or something. I said OK, we'll try this again. See, maybe this is kind of old-fashioned, but I still go with the idea that a family is a mom and a dad and kids, you know? And that's what we had. That's what we have.

"And all this Human Services bullshit about the kids . . . I didn't know what to think about that. I had no idea for a long time who was doing it. My mother wouldn't admit it. She'd been getting pretty churchy for a while. I'd lived with her for quite a few years, and I had never believed that her personality and Nancy's would mix that well. And the two personalities couldn't sit down and solve the problem. Nancy wanted to fix things between them for a while, but she doesn't want to solve it now. That's what I said twelve years ago. I told her, just stay away from her.

"After Nancy came back home, she talked to me about the real estate course, the classes and the test, she asked if I'd help her. I said sure, because I thought she'd be good at it. And it was a good idea for her not to go back to work at the bar again. That bullshit had to be over.

"She really applied herself, studied hard, and I think she probably had it nailed. She wouldn't have had any problem with that test. But then we had another stroke of bad luck that we needed right at that time.

"My first thought was to make sure she wasn't injured, that he hadn't hurt her physically. At that point, I didn't stop to think about the psychological stuff much. You get that later.

"It was a real bad time. She didn't sleep well—I woke up one night and she was beating me in the face. She wouldn't come downstairs by herself at night. She was real spooky about going anywhere by herself. And she was real mistrustful, and she'd never been like that before, not as long as I'd known her. Me, I don't trust anybody, and I don't believe anybody, not unless I can corroborate it, prove it myself. But Nancy always trusted people about everything. Not anymore.

"Going to the paper like we did . . . well, I thought maybe, somehow, it would do some good. Maybe this is finally something that society's ready to take a look at, do something about. It's one thing, though, when you're just sitting around talking about the issue of rape. It's another when it comes to your house. It's hard.

"Sure I thought about killing him. What with going to the different hearings, and the trial, there were times I was close enough. Nobody was paying much attention to me, they were all either watching Nancy or watching Bobby Lee Smith. Nobody ever checked me for weapons. I wasn't frisked, there weren't any metal detectors. It would've been no problem. I thought about it, once or twice. . . ."

"Nancy told me that she loved Steve, that she wanted him to quit abusing alcohol," says Bill Olson. "She really believed that the Mt. Pleasant hospitalization would prove it, that it was a tough-love step for his sake as well as hers, and it would serve to protect their marriage.

"The Human Services reports, and our injunction, came long before that. Nancy had come to me and said, 'What can I do to protect myself from my mother-in-law?' So I talked to the police and the social workers at Human Services. The reports required under law had essentially determined that none of the three abuse charges were 'founded.' They found nothing to make anyone believe that either Nancy or Steve were abusing those children.

"So we got the injunction. It doesn't say that Wilma can't travel, or use the telephone, or go any particular place, or live a normal life. It simply says that she cannot communicate with Nancy or the children. And that's when I started hearing from Wilma.

"I was convinced, based upon the writings that I had, including notes that she left at the office, and telephone messages that she left, that Wilma felt she should include me in her mission of converting the world to the idea that Nancy was abusing the children. The Department of Human Services, which gets paid for this, said there was no abuse. So I refused to talk to her.

"After the ongoing problems with Wilma, and after Steve's hospitalization, Nancy then came to me about the divorce. She wasn't particularly communicative about the underlying causes, I think she assumed I knew. Basically, all she told me was, 'I can't take this anymore.' I knew a lot about the troubles they'd been having, but I didn't know in any direct way about another man, and she didn't tell me. The street told me. It's too easy to be judgmental. I tried not to be.

"I think it was all about taking control of her life, even when it looked like she was out of control. It was about the constant frustration of having things happen *to* her. The injunction was about not living in a situation where people would seek to take control of her life and her children. Steve's hospitalization was, 'My life is being screwed up because my husband is drinking too much, and I want to take control of it.' The divorce was the same kind of thing. Even moving to Oklahoma, she wanted to be in charge of her life down there, but the person she turned to for assistance was her ex-husband, not the guy she'd gone down there with. That's when, I think, she began to figure it all out.

"When she came back to town, she came by the office and dropped off another twenty-five bucks on her account, as usual. And she said, 'Tell Bill I'm back home, and I'm living with Steven.' Between being a deacon in my church and being an attorney in my town, I see a lot of the way life is. I was glad she came home.

"And when she did, I thought back to the day when Steve had finally come to my office to sign the divorce agreement. He came in here, and sat in the conference room, and looked at that paper, and looked at it some more, without saying anything. And then he took a deep breath and shook his head, and said, 'All right, I'll sign the goddamn thing. But it doesn't mean I don't still love her.' And then he signed the paper and handed it to me and walked out of the office."

CHAPTER FIFTEEN

MANY PEOPLE'S LIVES—in fact, most people's lives, I'd guess—aren't tidy. Maybe we grew up watching Donna Reed and June Cleaver solve all the problems in their families in a half hour (and of course, those two tidy ladies never had any problems of their own), but we all know that's not real life. Negotiating your way around and through the messes we make, that's what real life is about. And finding some peace and happiness between your messes, if you're lucky.

So there we were, me and Steven and our family, trying to get through our own mess during the hot, tense, and endless summer of 1989. I baby-sat the kids at my house, went to flea markets on weekends with my mother, and answered the *Des Moines Register* reporter's questions. For hours, Jane Schorer would ask for whatever details I could dredge up, about when I was raped, and how I was raped, and what I did after my rape. I was caught between trying to remember those details and trying to forget them. For hours I would answer her, with time out for one or both of us to cry at the story I was telling.

I still jumped when the phone rang, or when someone knocked at the screen door. Steven had been saving up his vacation time to be with me at the trial, so there was no way the two of us could take a day or two and just get away; we had to stay home and stick with our routine. We got up every morning, and coped all day, and we'd go to bed at night, hoping for sleep. And in the morning, we'd get up and start all over again.

In early August, Bobby Lee Smith and Lisa Davis were married. We'd found out that he had five children, from twelve years of age to two, so maybe getting married made sense to him at that point. But what did this marriage mean to me, and to my case? I thought about all those old black-and-white movies on television, where the wife doesn't have to testify against the husband—did this mean Lisa didn't have to testify against him? No, Nan Horvat reassured me. The events she must testify to happened before their marriage.

But then the trial that was supposed to begin on August 23, for the kidnapping and rape of the Indianola woman, got rescheduled. One of the defense witnesses would not be available, Roger Owens said. So that trial went to October 18, and my trial got continued once again, to sometime in December.

It occurred to me that by the time I finally got my day in court, I would have celebrated my first anniversary as a rape victim. Some anniversary. One whole year of holidays, birthdays, and seasons changing. And Steven and I fought about taking a vacation. He was angry, and he had a point—he badly needed the break, and so did I. But a world in which normal people took normal vacations seemed as foreign and as far away as Mars.

After Labor Day, Nick and Ben went back to school, Sissy went off to preschool. And there still had been no break in the summer-long drought.

Lisa Davis Smith's trial for theft of my rings was scheduled for September 13, and I would have to testify. A few days before court, I reshuffled my day-care kids so that I could go into Des Moines with Steven and have my first day in court. It wouldn't be the "big" day, but it would, at last, be a beginning.

Then Nan called to head us off. Lisa Davis Smith had pleaded guilty to a lesser charge, which meant she now wouldn't have to go on trial. And I wouldn't have to testify.

I felt like a tennis ball, and the legal system was swinging both rackets. We kept arranging our lives, and our emotional energy, around one date, and then they'd bounce the date, and then we'd bounce, and then they'd bounce the date again. I was lighting one cigarette off another, and eating chocolate as if I thought somebody was going to wrestle it away from me. The justice system felt like the kids' Nintendo games. Somebody was programming the moves for the little people on the screen, but it wasn't me.

I couldn't stand to watch television—it was too hard to sit still, to pay attention. I'd lose track of who the characters were, and why they were important. The sitcoms didn't make me laugh, and everything else seemed to be about crime, and criminals, and victims. I decided I had to find some way to get out of my house.

I started going bowling on Friday nights with my girlfriends. It felt great to roll the ball down the alley and slam the pins. It even felt OK to throw a gutter ball once in a while—it gave me a good laugh on myself, and it gave me an excuse to jump up and down and make a lot of noise. Sometimes we'd all go out afterward for a drink, and I could almost pretend that life was as simple as spares and strikes.

I read in the local newspaper that there was going to be a guest lecturer at Grinnell College, a Professor Ruth Gresham from Ohio State. She was a counselor for victims of rape on that campus, and she would be holding a seminar for Grinnell students. When I called for more information, I found out that the lecture would be sponsored by the Office of Minority Students, and its director, Eric Wynn, told me I was welcome to attend. He was very kind over the phone, so I asked if it would be OK if I could speak to Ms. Gresham for a few minutes alone. Mr. Wynn said he would make arrangements for me to do so.

When I went into his office, I was startled to see that Eric Wynn was a black man. When he put out his hand to shake mine, I was very aware of my hand going out, being touched and shaken by his. He was the first black man I'd seen since the last hearing at the courthouse, when Bobby Lee Smith was there, and the only one I'd spoken to since the rape. My heart was thudding. I knew in my brain the response made little sense. I kept saying to myself, this is a nice man, this is a nice man.

I went into the conference room alone with Ms. Gresham. I explained my situation to her, and told her I wasn't quite sure what I wanted, but I felt somehow that she could help me. She gave me names and addresses of organizations that I hadn't discovered yet, and confirmed the information that I'd found on my own in the library. She also told me something else: that I was not a rape victim, but a rape survivor, who had not allowed my attacker to reduce me to "just a statistic." For whatever reason, I had found a way to keep going. Maybe, she suggested, I should think of passing on what I was learning to others, to help them make the transition from victim to survivor, too. The words she said to me in private gave me much to think about a few minutes later, as she began to speak to the others who came to hear her lecture.

Dee Ann Wolfe had driven from Des Moines to attend the seminar, and Diane Pickens came, too. We all sat up in the front row, and I was a little surprised to look over and see Wilma Ziegenmeyer. I was even more surprised—no, stunned—when she stood up and shared her story of the sexual and physical abuse she'd experienced in her family when she was a child.

When I got home that night, I told Steven all about the evening's events. He was sad and uncomfortable about the stuff about his mother, and didn't want to talk much about what I'd heard. But he did have an opinion about what Ruth Gresham had told me.

I'd been a prisoner of my own pain and frustration for nearly a year, he said, and except for that night with Cathy Burnham, and a few group counseling sessions, I had hardly been able to get outside my own head. But it *had* been nearly a year, which put me a little bit ahead of someone whose own hell might be just beginning today. Maybe, Steven said, helping that victim to become a survivor would be the best way to turn all of this into something positive. It was something to consider.

At the end of September, another phone call from Nan Horvat. Another continuance of our case, the fourth one. We were now rescheduled for January 22. Now we'd gone into 1990. Another year.

It was the DNA, Nan told me. Roger Owens and Cynthia Moisan wanted their own scientific experts to run another set of tests, but the FBI was still dragging their feet about cooperating. In my mind, I had a clear picture of the FBI guys dressed in their suits, literally dragging their wingtips behind them through the mud, clutching in their sweaty little hands the very thing that might get us all into court and get this done with.

Once again I yelled at Nan, and then yelled at Steven. I yelled at the children, and yelled at my friends. At least my rapist just did it once, I told them. He didn't keep coming back and doing it over and over again, like the justice system did, and the FBI, and maybe even the scientific experts. I had little faith in experts—I had decided that an expert was just some guy from out of state who wears a suit and carries a briefcase.

It was just a game to all of them, I cried. Or maybe it's what they do between nine and five every day. They did it before I got raped, they'll do it to the next woman who gets attacked, and to hell with the person at the center of it. I was just another victim on their list—the bottom of their list.

I had always been for the death penalty. The best thing for these guys, I had always said back in the good old days of my ignorance, is just to get rid of them. But now, I was slowly beginning to change my mind. As one day dragged into another, and the weeks into months, and I saw my life more and more in the control of others, I thought: No, dying's too good for him. Let him sit, like I do, and wait. Let him sit and wait for the rest of his life.

Nan Horvat: "This was the third time we'd used DNA in an Iowa criminal trial, and I had every reason to believe it would be the third time we'd bring in a guilty verdict using DNA. I tried to explain to Nancy that back when fingerprinting was just beginning to be used, it was challenged in exactly the same way by the courts. Yet now, we take it for granted that fingerprints can be introduced as evidence. The same thing happened when we started using gunshot residue analysis—defense lawyers challenged it as ridiculous, and now we use it all the time. One day, we'll take the use of DNA analysis for granted in exactly the same way.

"I was satisfied with what the FBI labs had come up with, but Roger and Cindy didn't trust it. They wanted a chance for their own experts to run the tests and then testify, and the FBI seemed to be ignoring our motions to produce. The judge could've said, 'Get on with it, go with what you've got,' but he didn't. I understood Nancy's increasing anger and frustration—I was getting pretty angry myself. I wanted to get this trial going. But I have to admit, there was a night or two when I called my friend Dee Ann Wolfe and said, 'Help, I need a crisis counselor! I just got off the phone with Ziegenmeyer!' "

Roger Owens: "I told Nan I thought the whole DNA thing was hocus-pocus, that she didn't even need it for this case, but if the prosecution insisted on introducing what their expert said, then the defense was going to get our own expert, and introduce whatever he said. Of course, I could probably bring in a palm reader and get him qualified as an expert. . . .

"One of the problems, of course, is that there is no standard testing procedure from one lab to another. And the labs all guard their secrets—they don't want to tell anyone how they do what they do. So when it seemed they were keeping secrets from us, it was really about these labs keeping secrets from each other. The combination of the feds and the scientists . . . it's lethal stuff.

"I know Nancy Ziegenmeyer saw the system as responsible for these delays. I'd have been just as happy without 'em myself. But Bobby wasn't running loose at that point, he wasn't out on bail or anything. He was locked up in jail the whole time. How is she hurt, how is the system hurt, by making sure he gets a fair trial?"

On October 18, 1989, Bobby Lee Smith's trial on charges of raping and kidnapping the young woman from Indianola began in Des Moines, with Nan Horvat prosecuting for the state of Iowa, and Roger Owens for the defense.

I had such mixed emotions about it. I knew so well what that woman had gone through. I had asked Dee Ann Wolfe about her, and she'd told me that not only did she not have the kind of family support I'd had, she'd abruptly stopped using the support resources at the crisis center in Des Moines.

Dee Ann didn't betray any confidences, but what little she could tell me made me very sad. It sounded as if the only place this woman would find justice would be in the courtroom, that her only hope was that the verdict would go in her favor, that Smith be found guilty.

On the other hand (and I was finding out that there was *always* an other hand), if he was found guilty of this one, "my" trial would never happen. I sat by the phone and filled up ashtrays all that day, and all the next.

On October 19, one month short of the first anniversary of my rape, the jury found Bobby Lee Smith not guilty of the charges. I heard the news with a sick stomach. She sat there and told them he did it, and they didn't believe her. What if they didn't believe me either? It was just one more good news/ bad news joke. The bad news: He got off. The good news: Now it's our turn.

CHAPTER SIXTEEN

JANE SCHORER told me that there would be a meeting of the Iowa Freedom of Information Council in Des Moines at the end of October. Geneva Overholser would be one of the people on the panel, and the topic for discussion that night would be how the news media cover crime, and how their coverage affects the lives of the victims of those crimes. There would be reporters there, and police, and lawyers. I asked Steven if he'd take me.

Once again, I sat in the front row and listened to someone speak as an "expert" about what happens to crime victims. They talked about confidentiality versus the need to keep people informed. They talked about what was good for society versus what is good or helpful for the victim. I squirmed and fidgeted, and dug my fingers into Steven's leg. We'd seen the news items in the *Des Moines Register* about Bobby Lee Smith's trials, his acquittal in the first case, the use of DNA in the upcoming second trial. Neither the Indianola woman nor I was named in the paper, but nevertheless, it was a shock to see the details of our lives in print at the breakfast table every morning.

I listened to the speakers go on and on about their "theoretical" victim. To me, the more they talked, the stupider they sounded. Granted, they might know how to be reporters, or editors, or lawyers, or cops. But how could they know what it was like to be a victim? What do they know about it, I mumbled. Steven looked over at me. I'll give them their "theoretical" victim, I thought, and almost without knowing I was about to do it, I raised my hand and stood up.

There, standing in front of about a hundred people I didn't know, I heard with astonishment the words coming out of my own mouth. "I am a rape victim."

The room was very quiet. There were eyes on me like there had been that first morning in Mercy Hospital's emergency room, but this was different. As I told them, from beginning to end, what had happened, and how everything having to do with it had made me feel, they listened. I was unsure of myself and my role here, and I rushed the words out. Then I'd stop to take a shaky breath, then begin to rush the words out again. I knew that what I was saying was important for them to hear. And I knew it was important to me to say it.

I guess it took about four or five minutes, and then I was done. I didn't feel victorious, but I didn't feel defeated, either. Mostly, I felt relieved. There, I said to myself. There.

I sat down at about the same time my legs decided to fold up under me, and I reached over for Steven's hand. And then we heard it—those people were clapping their hands.

Geneva Overholser, editor of the *Des Moines Register*, remembers very well the first day she met Nancy and Steven Ziegenmeyer.

"They sat right here in my office, and they were very nervous. But that kind of bubbly energy of Nancy's was evident immediately. Also evident was a lack of really knowing what, precisely, they were getting into. She didn't literally come in here and say use my name, tell my story. She said that she had been reading a lot of things—and I remember she had a notebook with her. It was clear that here was a rape victim who was not trying to obliterate or deny anything. This was a woman who was getting into it. And I thought to myself, this is maybe a very healthy thing.

"Earlier that summer, the Supreme Court had ruled on a case where a Florida newspaper had used the name of a rape victim. The victim had sued for damages, and she'd won, but the Supreme Court overturned the original verdict. A friend of mine at the *New York Times*, where I'd once worked, was writing a piece on that decision and about the impact on the media of the constitutionality of using—or not using—victims' names. And he called and asked for my thoughts about this.

"As a feminist, I've always cared deeply about the issue of rape, and about the issue of all violence against women. But as a journalist, I had not really, consciously sorted out the issue of confidentiality versus the nature of the crime. I don't think, at that point, that a lot of people in the business had. So I made a few off-the-cuff remarks about my feelings, about this uncharacteristic quality we had, as journalists, to withhold victims' names in this one crime. And these remarks showed up in the *New York Times* piece.

"Then an editor of the op-ed page of the *Times* called and asked if I wanted to write a piece for them, going into these issues in more depth. I said I'd be glad to, but I didn't want to write one for the *New York Times* and not have it run in the *Des Moines Register*, too. After all, this is my paper. So I wrote it, and we ran it in the *Register*, and I thought, well, it's really sort of arcane, and our readers probably aren't going to give a hoot about this. And then Nancy called.

"My impression was that this was an articulate person, a rape victim who also saw herself as a victim of the justice system. I thought it would be a very interesting profile, but I said I wanted her to think very carefully about feeling comfortable with this. She said that in the months since the rape she'd come to feel twice violated. I wanted her to make an informed decision before letting herself in for anything that might make her even more vulnerable.

"Once Nancy thought it all over and decided she wanted to go ahead, I went to the features desk and talked about finding a reporter for this. I was certainly conscious that while Nancy had very strong feelings, and voiced them beautifully, this was a story in which we'd have to do extensive reporting, with the courts, with the police . . . it was such a loaded issue, after all.

"Once Jane Schorer had been assigned the story, I would check in with her every once in a while, just to see how it was going. They talked almost daily, I think, and Jane kept up with all the twists and turns in the court system.

"We made a number of judgment calls about what this story was and, therefore, what it was not. It was not, for instance, a balanced portrayal of the crime itself. As you can imagine, my editors said to me, why don't you have more in here about Bobby Lee Smith? Why don't you have more in here about the crime of rape on a national level? But we said, in the title, what it was: 'One Woman's Story.'

"We were enormously fortunate in several regards. One, that Nancy was so articulate and courageous. Unswervingly forthright with Jane. Two, that while it was a terrible thing that had happened, it was a crime that we could describe with some accuracy of detail without the graphic . . . well, for instance, there was a rape here about the time of Nancy's that was just unspeakably horrible. The woman was badly beaten, abused in every reprehensible way, in the fetal position for weeks afterward in the hospital, without being able to speak. That's not to get into a comparison of whose rape is worse, or where a rape falls on a scale of one to ten. But a reader coming to those kinds of details would have had great difficulty getting past the horror to the woman at the heart of the story.

"Someone said to me that I should've waited, for years if necessary, for a rape in which they were both of the same race, so that race would not be an issue. Well, I could've waited my whole career for a story that could be told as this one was and for a victim who wanted to tell it. I didn't feel that race was an issue here. It was pertinent information to the police, in terms of trying to find her attacker, but it wasn't pertinent to the victim and what she went through.

"The journalism world is struggling with whether or not to

identify rape victims. It doesn't matter if the rapist is black or white, or if the victim knew him or not, the question we're asking is, Should we be identifying her?

"The second question is whether society is focusing on violence against women. I don't think we are—not in any meaningful way. Crimes against women are folded into the larger category of crime statistics, yet when you break them out, they're a hugely disproportionate share of that larger number.

"For years, when we as a culture have looked at rape, we've looked at it in salacious ways, rather than in public policy–directed ways. We should be asking what's wrong with this picture, and what needs changing? I wanted readers to focus on a crime they don't want to focus on, to think about rape, and to think about it as a crime that happens primarily to women.

"Often, my double fervors of journalism and feminism are at odds with each other, I do battle over which side to come down on. This time, they worked together. And this time, the reader could not say, well, that's too awful for me to look at.

"Some people said, oh, you just want to sell newspapers. Well, sure, that's the business I'm in—I mean, if we don't sell newspapers, we won't have newspapers. That's just the logic of the marketplace. But the fact is, the things that sell newspapers are mostly interesting things. Nancy Ziegenmeyer afforded us the opportunity to present a woman and a story readers could not reject."

CHAPTER SEVENTEEN

ANOTHER WINTER, with short dark days, and long cold nights, and freezing wind blowing around outside our house at about a million miles an hour. Another Thanksgiving. Another Christmas. My blood pressure was sky-high, and my disposition was at swamp-bottom level. The children were jumping around, bouncing from room to room with that incredible energy kids have once the toy commercials start blaring on television, and neither Steven nor I had much patience for it. There were so many things I wanted back in my life, not the least of which was the way it used to feel around our house during the holidays.

One night I dreamed I had a meeting with Iowa's attorney general, Tom Miller. In the dream I talked him into hiring me to run a new victims' rights program. When I woke up, I enthusiastically told Steven all about the dream. He admired me for my ambitious subconscious—or was it my unconscious?—but said that, since he himself felt mostly like killing somebody these days, it was likely that our two goals would cancel each other out.

Nan Horvat called to tell us that Bobby Lee Smith had written to the judge asking that somebody please set a court date and get on with the trial. In his letter, he talked about his wife and children, and how they needed him, and how he wanted to get off this "emotional roller coaster." I never thought I'd agree with anything Bobby Lee Smith had to say, but this was one time we were both thinking alike.

There was another hearing before the court about the DNA evidence. Steven and I drove into Des Moines for it and sat in the back of the room listening as the scientific "experts" went back and forth with the three attorneys about what would or would not be admitted into evidence.

I tried to pay close attention to what they were all saying, but sometimes the science stuff was as thick as mud to me no matter how much I wanted to understand it. I got distracted, and found myself watching the attorneys in a different way, almost as if they were characters in a play.

Nan, for instance, was almost always calm and composed. My Gramma would've called her ladylike, which is her highest compliment. She's very pretty, but not flashy. She always dressed in a way that said it was okay to notice what she was wearing, thank you very much, but she'd rather that you paid attention to what she was saying. When I first met her, she had seemed almost delicate to me, but I had learned over the months that she had iron ore for backbone, and didn't like anybody pushing her around. Every time Roger leaned on her, she leaned back, in a neat, deliberate way. I'll bet, if I ever invited Nan to my house, that she'd want to straighten the pictures on the walls. She'd probably be too polite to do it while I was in the room, but once I left, she'd do it.

Roger, on the other hand, was never calm. He didn't yell exactly, but his voice, his way of talking, was large—when he was talking, you sat up and paid attention, for different reasons than when you paid attention to Nan. He seemed restless, like someone whose motor is running even when he's sitting still. His face would flush up when he got mad, like Steven's does, and he would roll his eyes whenever he got disgusted at what he heard. At first Roger didn't seem as sharp, as smart somehow, as Nan, but I had watched him closely, and finally decided that was a disguise. If I ever invited Roger to my house, he'd probably spill something on purpose and then, when I left the room to get a paper towel, he'd quickly lean over and read all the mail on my desk.

Cynthia Moisan—Steven always called her "The Ice Queen"—was on the defense team primarily for her expertise with DNA evidence. Whenever she spoke up, it was in very technical language, discussing the scientific methods used, how long they had been used, the ways they were and were not reliable. She was very precise, and she had her stuff down cold. At each hearing and during the trial, she was dressed like something out of a fashion magazine, very elegant and stylish. I always had this urge to check my makeup whenever I saw her. She and Roger were an odd couple, and they were beginning to scare the hell out of me. I thought of them as Bobby Lee Smith's firepower.

My attention was brought back to the hearing by Hal Deadman, the FBI expert, who kept referring to DNA material taken from "the victim's panties." Hearing him say the word *panties* just set my teeth on edge. It was another damn step over some invisible line everyone kept crossing, to hear that word used over and over. That was me he was talking about, and my underwear.

During a break, I asked Nan if she could please ask Mr. Deadman to use "underwear" instead of "panties." She agreed to do it, and "underwear" it mostly was for the rest of the hearing and on into the trial.

The presiding judge, Anthony Critelli, was brusque and short-tempered with all of them that day. I later learned he'd just come from being a pall-bearer at his best friend's funeral. He sharply reminded them that Bobby Lee Smith, although still presumed innocent of any crime, had now spent almost a year in jail waiting for the lawyers to quit nit-picking over evidence.

Smith was in the courtroom. Steven and I both stared and stared at him, willing him to look up at us, just once. But he never did.

In spite of the way we were both feeling, we resolved on the

way home to at least try to do the best we could with the
children throughout the holidays. It wasn't fair to let their
Christmas be spoiled by something they, and we, had no
control over. And maybe their laughter and general silliness
this time of year was something we could both use. Maybe
Christmas spirit was something you could catch from your
kids.

So I watched a couple of the TV specials with them, and we
made cookies, and Steven and I once again went shopping for
their presents. I took out the boxes of decorations and spruced
up the house, which was more than I'd done the year before.
And, of course, we took them to Christmas dinner at Gramma
and Grampa's. But I felt I was moving through my life like
some kind of zombie. When New Year's Eve came and 1989
rolled over into 1990, it meant only one thing: the trial.

Shortly before the court date, Nan told me she didn't want
me to sit in the courtroom during the actual trial itself. I would
just come in and give my testimony, and then Roger Owens
would cross-examine me; after that, she wanted me out of the
room.

I protested noisily. After all this time, I couldn't believe she
wouldn't let me take a front-row seat. But Nan held her
ground. She explained that if the jurors saw me calmly sitting
there day after day, without showing any signs of being afraid
of the man who would be just across the room from me, then
maybe they would forget about my testimony, about how
frightened I had been in the car that day—about how I truly
believed that he was going to kill me. In a way, my presence
could make them immune to me. It would be better to come
in, tell my story, and then leave.

Her argument had some logic to it, so I reluctantly agreed.
Steven, on the other hand, announced that he was planning to
sit in the goddamn courtroom, all day, every day, until it was
over, no matter how long it lasted, and there wasn't a goddamn
thing Nan Horvat or anybody else could do about it. No one

argued with him. He said he'd come out and tell me what was going on. Jane Schorer would be sitting in during the trial, too, so I'd have two sources of information.

A few days into the new year, news came from Boston that a man named Charles Stuart had thrown himself off a bridge into the icy Charles River. Stuart had accused a black man of robbing him and his wife, then shooting them both. Mrs. Stuart had died, along with their unborn child, and Charles Stuart himself had almost died from his gunshot wound. The whole city of Boston was in turmoil about it. Now it turned out that Stuart had lied. He had apparently done it all himself, and there never had been any black assailant, or any assailant at all.

The story raised again all the old issues of race, and racism, and crime, and prejudice. Somebody brought up the "wilding" attack on the Central Park jogger in New York, comparing the accusations in the two cases. It was all over the papers, it was on television, it was in the weekly newsmagazines, and everybody was talking about it—and asking me what I thought. It was strangely creepy, and it made me feel like I had to defend my own accusation. This was getting ridiculous: A murderous man I didn't even know, who lived half a country away, could make me feel guilty about being a rape victim, about accusing a man who just happened to be black of being my rapist. But the Stuart case doesn't have anything in common with my case, I told anyone who asked. And I'm not the one who brought race into this, I kept saying. He did.

One night Cathy Burnham and I drove into Des Moines to go to a group support session at Polk County Victim Services. My mom came over to sit with the children and fix dinner for them and Steven after he got home from work.

After the session, as Cathy and I headed home, we talked about how much these meetings meant to us, how safe we felt sitting in a room with women who had gone through the same thing we had. It was such a relief not having to explain every feeling we had, every day we couldn't function, every night we couldn't sleep. It was a comfort to know that behavior that was weird or crazy to everyone else was perfectly understandable to them. And Cathy told me her nightmares had stopped. She hadn't had a bad dream for months.

When we got home, my mom told us that there had been a telephone call for Steven, just before he'd gotten home from work. The caller had said he was a lawyer in Grinnell, and gave her his name, but he didn't leave a number or any additional message. He just hung up. That's strange, we thought. Our number had been unlisted for months, and I couldn't imagine where this guy had gotten it. Bill Olson wouldn't have passed on our number to anyone without checking with us, I was sure of it.

A few minutes later, the telephone rang again. I answered it, and heard a man's voice on the other end. I didn't recognize it, and when he asked for Steven, I handed the phone to him.

"Meet me at nine-thirty tonight in front of the Grinnell State Bank," the man said quickly, and then hung up.

Steven stood there for a minute with the phone in his hand, and then he called the local police. It was too close to the trial date for us not to take this seriously—it was clear that somebody was playing some kind of scary game to get him to leave the house. When the police checked, there was no one in front of the bank. The next day, we pulled the kids out of school.

We called Ralph Roth in Des Moines and told him what had happened and what our fears were. After he spoke with the local police, he requested and got a tap on our phone. My rapist had made threats against my family. Now that we were approaching an actual trial, there was every reason to believe that those threats would be carried out.

Each morning for nearly a week, after Steven left for work, I would draw the drapes closed, shove the deadbolt lock on the front door, and sit around the television with the children all day. It was like the first weeks after the rape, and all the same fear and pain came rushing back. I couldn't go to the grocery store, I couldn't answer the phone, and I insisted that all three kids stay within sight. Whenever one of them disappeared upstairs, or into the bathroom, I'd panic and go off looking, calling their names.

At first they all thought it was some kind of unplanned vacation, but a day or two into it, they hated it. They were bored with television, bored with my paranoia, and jumpy from staying inside waiting for—what? I sure didn't know, and neither did anybody else.

On January 18, another continuance was granted, moving the trial again, this time to January 24. Something about the DNA again, the defense's expert witnesses. I couldn't absorb the details anymore, and what difference would it have made, anyway? It was the fifth continuance, and the end of the road for any tolerance or patience I might have had left. My birthday would fall on the twenty-ninth. I would, in all likelihood, spend my twenty-ninth birthday sitting in the hallway outside the courtroom, waiting for the people inside to decide when and if I could ever come up for air.

"To hell with it. I quit. I'm not going to testify!" I announced to Nan Horvat. Take that, I thought!

Her response was terse. "That's just fine, Nancy," she said to me, "don't testify. It's not like I don't have other things I could be doing. I'll call the judge to let him know, and we'll just cancel the whole thing. And then that will be the end of it."

I don't know what I had expected her to do when I threatened to back out—although it felt good to say it—but the idea of the whole thing somehow evaporating wasn't what I wanted either.

At the end of the week, we reluctantly let the children go back to school. It was better for them to be busy and occupied in their own world than to continue to be held hostage with me in mine.

CHAPTER EIGHTEEN

WEDNESDAY, JANUARY 24, 1990. We had set the alarm, but we were both awake long before it went off. Outside, the snow was falling fast and heavily, and there were high winds. A blizzard. Interstate 80 would be a sloppy mess, and we would have to leave early to get to the courthouse on time.

Trying to find omens anywhere I could, I checked out my horoscope in the *Des Moines Register* while Steven made the coffee. It read: "Energy focused on preparatory activities. Subconscious thoughts could lead to revelation. Consider psychology as a profession."

Preparatory activities? Well, that fit—they'd be doing jury selection today. That's pretty good, I thought as I put the paper away. It could have been worse.

We left the house at around 6:30. There was no way I could do the driving—the combination of the bad weather and my sheer terror at what was finally beginning put Steven into the driver's seat and me into the passenger seat, chain-smoking and wringing a handkerchief into a twisted knot.

Steven's driving like a farmer, I thought. He looked carefully to the left and to the right, moving through the storm as if he were driving a tractor. He approached each intersection with caution, and pulled way over to the right whenever someone behind us wanted to pass. He commented on the weather, the scenery, the other drivers. I wanted to scream at him.

We were listening to KJJY when they broke in with the headlines on the hour. "Jury selection to begin today for trial on charges of kidnapping and rape of Grinnell woman. DNA, controversial genetic fingerprinting technique, to be presented in evidence. Defendant found not guilty in previous trial."

We had closely followed the coverage of the previous trial in the *Des Moines Register,* of course, and had watched carefully as that coverage shifted to the court's preparations for this trial. But that had not prepared us for having those same headlines jump out at us in a booming male voice inside our own car. I'd been a lot of things in the past months. victim, survivor, witness. This was the first time I realized something new had been added to the list. Now I was news.

As agreed, I was prepared to stay out in the corridor during the proceedings like a good girl. But after everything got going inside, I planned to just casually go up and peek through the glass in the door and hope no one noticed me. Steven went into the courtroom and sat down. The seating area for observers was very small—only one bench about fifteen feet long, like a church pew. Steven quickly saw that he would be sitting very close to Bobby Lee Smith's family members; his parents, brothers, wife, and children. Jane Schorer would also be inside the courtroom for the whole trial, taking notes for the *Des Moines Register* story, and David Peterson, the *Register's* photographer, would be trying to get pictures. He wasn't going to be able to take his camera equipment into the courtroom, so he'd have to manage as best he could from the hallway, discreetly taking shots with a long lens through the glass in the door.

Dee Ann Wolfe had come to sit in the hall with me. We watched throughout the morning as people filed in and out of the courtroom, and Nan, Roger, and Judge Arthur Gamble went through the process of choosing the jurors who would ultimately decide this case. All of this rests in your hands, in your hearts, I silently said to them. More than the lawyers, or the police, or even the judge, you have all the power now. Please, oh, please, use it wisely.

Ralph Roth, who had been out of town for a while, dropped by to cheer me on. He sat and talked with us for a few minutes, and as always, something in his voice, something in his face, gave me reason to hope. We walked down the hallway and had a cigarette together, and I laughed to remember that first day at the hospital, when I'd sponged cigarettes from him. He had believed in me from the beginning, and it was that belief that had started me on this road more than a year ago.

By lunchtime, all twelve members of the jury had been picked. There were six men and six women. The jury was all white. One of the alternates was black.

We went to lunch, but I mostly pushed my food around the plate until it was time to go back to the courthouse.

In the afternoon, there was some confusion about Lisa Davis Smith and her testimony. She took the stand to testify, and then claimed her Fifth Amendment right not to say anything. The only way, Nan told me later, that we could get her to tell the story about the rings was to grant her immunity from prosecution. So that's what they did. She'd been part of all of this all along, I thought, but now nothing would happen to her. Another piece of the justice puzzle that made a big picture I didn't understand.

As it grew later, it was clear that I wouldn't be testifying that day. The judge sent everyone home until nine the next morning, and Steven and I slowly made the trip back to Grinnell— but not before we stopped and picked up some chocolate for me.

When we got in the door, the children greeted us. "Are you all done, Mommy?" they asked. "Did they put the bad guy in jail?" I had to explain to them that no, we weren't done yet, we were just at the beginning of being done. We were all too spoiled by TV, where there was an arrest, a trial, and a verdict, all in an hour, minus time for commercials. This, I explained to them, was real life, and so it would take a little longer.

The next morning we once again woke up before the alarm went off. Today I would get my turn, I thought. Today I get to point my finger.

All my life—I admit it—I've been vain. I like to have my hair look nice, and my nails done, and my clothes just so. I like to buy clothes and I like to wear them, and I like to take my time getting ready to go out. It's something that has always driven Steven nuts, for it often leaves him downstairs waiting while I'm still upstairs putting on the finishing touches. But this one morning I wouldn't have known if my stockings were full of holes and my coat was on backwards. Weeks before, I'd picked out my good black suit to wear, but today, I could've worn my bathrobe to court and not been aware of it. I'd been waiting for what seemed like a lifetime for this one day. Now that it was here, all I felt was sick.

Way above our heads, high up on the west wall of the central rotunda of the courthouse, there were some lines written. "Law is the science in which the greatest powers of the understanding are applied to the greatest number of facts." It was by someone named B. Johnson. I wondered what B. Johnson knew about wanting to throw up in these hallowed halls, wanting to shout and yell like a crazy person, wanting to turn and run.

Dee Ann and Nan walked me down the hall into the courtroom. I was hanging on to them, and my knees were shaking so much I thought people would see. We had been here before—Nan had brought me in one day to show me where I would sit, where the jury would be, and where Bobby Lee Smith and Roger Owens would sit. But this wasn't make-believe, I thought as I walked to my chair. Like I'd told the children the night before, this was real life.

I sat down and faced the room. Steven was sitting right there, looking at me. There was an expression on his face, in his eyes, that I had seen often over the past year, a combination of sadness and anger, and great weariness. He could not change what had happened to me, and he could not take the pain away, but he carried it around inside himself like some kind of cancer.

As Nan took me through the morning of the rape, question by question, sentence by sentence, she spoke slowly and carefully. I tried to answer in the same way. Sometimes I felt myself wanting to hurry through my answers and sometimes I felt myself not wanting to answer at all. At some point, I started crying.

"Is the person who did all these things to you, Nancy, in the courtroom here today?" she finally asked.

"Yes," I said.

"Can you point him out?" she asked.

This was the moment I'd waited for.

"He's the man sitting right there," and I pointed my finger at Bobby Lee Smith. I waited for the tight little knot in the pit of my stomach to relax. It didn't.

And then she went on. One by one, she held out pieces of clothing. State's Exhibit No. 1A: my dinosaur underpants. Exhibit No. 10: my jumper. Exhibit No. 11: my tights. Exhibit No. 12: my sweater. Exhibit No. 13: my denim jacket.

Then she took me through the time spent at the hospital, and the car ride around Des Moines with Ralph as we looked for the house with the numbers on it, and my identification of all the pictures. At the end, she asked, "At any time, did you give Bobby Smith permission to have sex with you?"

"No," I said in as strong a voice as I could.

"Thank you," she said, and then Judge Gamble said, "Cross-examination." Here it comes, I thought. I asked for a break.

I headed directly for Steven, and we went out into the hallway with Dee Ann. She went with me to the ladies room, then I got a drink of water, and a cigarette. I knew, when I went back into the courtroom, it would be Roger Owens's turn. What would he do to me? He'd already convinced one jury that Bobby Lee Smith hadn't raped the Indianola woman; what would he do to convince this jury that Bobby Lee Smith hadn't raped me?

Roger Owens began as quietly and carefully as Nan had done. He was polite, and asked my permission each time he approached me. Initially, his questions were about my picture identifications: when they were done, how they were done, how sure or unsure I had been each time. The differences between dark-complected black men and medium-complected black men. Bobby Lee Smith with glasses, Bobby Lee Smith without.

"The reason I picked these pictures was because of his face," I explained.

"What is it about his face?" Roger asked. "I know it's hard to explain, but maybe you can do that for me."

"Yeah," I said. "It's because I see his face. Every time I shut my eyes at night I see his face. I'll never forget it."

Once we got past the photo identifications, he played a nasty little trick on me with suits. I told him I'd touched the rapist's suit and remembered the way it had felt. So he asked me to close my eyes and touch the suits he would hand to me.

I didn't want to close my eyes—I was too aware of Bobby Lee Smith sitting only five or six feet away from me. But I did as he asked and felt the material of each of the suits he held out in front of me. I identified the one that felt most like what I'd felt in the car that morning. When I opened my eyes again, I saw that I'd identified Roger Owens's own suit.

Then he spent a few more minutes clearing up the time frame: when I'd gotten to Grand View, when the car door had opened, how long the rape had taken, when I'd gotten to the hospital. And then, it seemed, he was done. "Thank you," he said.

Then Nan came back, for what the judge called a redirect, clearing up once again the times of different events and the pictures. "Thank you," she said at the end.

And then Roger Owens came back once more, for a recross-examination—more questions about the picture identifications. And then, when he was satisfied, he said, for what I dearly hoped was the last time, "Thank you."

And then I heard the judge say, "Thank you, ma'am. You may step down."

I was shaking as I walked past the defense table where Smith was sitting. Was that it? Did I convince the jury? Was that all

Roger Owens was going to do to me? Where were all the questions about the divorce, about my behavior, about leaving my family and running off to Oklahoma? Wasn't somebody, sometime, going to throw all of that back into my face? I couldn't believe that was all that was going to happen. Yes, Nan told me, that was it.

Once again, we all went downtown for lunch, and once again, I pushed my food around my plate with my fork. Steven asked Dee Ann how she thought it had gone. I thought of a couple of places where I might have said something differently, to make my testimony better.

That afternoon, I sat out in the hallway, or walked up and down the corridor, as the other witnesses spoke inside the courtroom. Steven stayed inside the courtroom and heard the policeman who briefly interviewed me in the hospital before Ralph had. Then came the testimony of the woman from the pawnshop, where Ralph had found my rings.

And then Lisa Smith took the stand and told the story of my rings, and how she got them. Once again, she told the story of the Hispanic people at the Kwik-Shop, who had given her the rings in exchange for money they needed, because they were having car trouble. And then, Steven told me later, the lawyers and the judge went on and on at some length about Lisa's immunity: who had given it to her, and why, and what she thought it meant. Roger Owens and Nan evidently got into some kind of battle, and then the discussions got moved, outside the hearing of the jury. And then they came back and told Lisa Smith that although they were through with her for the time being, they might call her back later.

The last two witnesses were the policewoman who had dusted my car for prints and a fingerprint expert who had looked at the car after that, identifying the only print found in the car as mine. At a little after three that afternoon, the judge once again adjourned for the day and sent everyone home until the next morning.

We drove back to Grinnell again, me with chocolate in one

hand and a cigarette in the other, Steven with a beer. He told me everything that had gone on inside the courtroom, while I replayed my own testimony over and over again. Did I do it right? Was it OK? Would they believe me?

When we got home, the children asked, as they had the night before, if the bad guy had gone to prison yet. When I told them not yet, one of them asked, "But Mommy, how long is this going to take?" Steven and I just looked at each other over their heads. It was a question we couldn't answer. A parent's least favorite response to a child's question is "I don't know," but it was the only one, at that point, that we could give them.

CHAPTER NINETEEN

THE NEXT DAY WAS FRIDAY, January 26. Once again I sat restlessly in the corridor or walked up and down the hallways, watching the doors open and close, the people going in and out. During breaks, Steven would come out and get me caught up on who said what to whom.

It was only the third day, yet I felt as if I'd been there for weeks, and might be there for weeks more. I had started going into Helen Youngs's office, down at the end of the hall. She was the court clerk for the grand jury, and she always had candy on her desk. I'd sit there for a while, and smoke, and babble, and eat her candy, trying to get some sense from her if everything was going along the way it was supposed to. There were a couple of policemen out in the hall that I got to know, too. They were fellow smokers—these days, smokers are always glad to find other smokers. People were certainly being very nice to me, I thought.

I watched as Dr. Kees from Mercy Hospital went into court to testify about my examination, and then the lab technician, who had sent all the body sample material to the FBI. Cynthia Moisan, Steven later told me, did the cross-examination of the lab technician, and there were quite a few questions about DNA testing: how long it had been going on, how many laboratories in the country were doing the tests. It was clear that everything in the testimony having to do with DNA would probably raise a red flag for Ms. Moisan.

Ralph Roth testified next. Nan took him through all the details, from the first moment he spoke to me until the time Bobby Lee Smith was arrested. And then, of course, Roger cross-examined him. During the cross-examination, Steven said, Roger actually got up and walked back and forth in front of the jury, which is something neither he nor Nan had done so far—except for a few minutes when they were questioning me, they usually asked their questions while sitting down at their tables. Nan objected to Roger's pacing around like that.

It was only a little after 11:30 in the morning when Ralph finished testifying, but the judge excused everyone until the following Monday, "Have a nice weekend," he said. Fat chance, I thought.

As everyone was leaving, Roger Owens passed me and Steven.

"Mrs. Ziegenmeyer," he said, "I'm very sorry about what happened to you. But I'm just doing my job, defending Bobby Lee Smith."

A slight breeze down that hall would've blown me right over. I was too surprised to even speak. As I watched him walk away, I thought: This man has spooked me since the very beginning. He's the enemy. Isn't he? Now I'll have to think about the possibility that he's a human being. There were all kinds of things I had learned over the past year; this would be just one more to add to the list.

It was a long weekend for us. We did chores around the house, and I went to the market, where I discovered that Grinnell's gossip line had been working just fine. Between the stories in the newspapers and that fill-in-the-blanks thing that folks in small towns do, the word had finally gotten around, I could tell. People I hadn't told about the rape were treating me funny, looking at me in a different way, speaking to me in hushed voices as if somebody had died. Steven ran into a couple of guys from work, and they asked him how his vacation was going, knowing perfectly well he was not driving into Des Moines every day to amuse himself.

We tried to give the children the kind of attention they needed. But they were bad, bad, bad. They knew, with that intuition kids have, that Mommy was at the bottom of a pit and Daddy wasn't far behind, and they kept pushing us just as far as they could. One by one we took their privileges away. OK, no TV. OK, no dessert. OK, no Nintendo. Finally, we sent everybody off to bed early.

On Sunday night, going back to court the next morning was only the second big item on my list. My birthday was the first. I fell asleep thinking, tomorrow I'm old, old, old. Tomorrow I'll be twenty-nine, and the one after that is thirty, and after that, I might as well be dead.

The next morning all my new friends at the courthouse wished me a happy birthday. There were greetings from Nan, and from Helen Youngs. Jane Schorer gave me a gift—a nice, new "granny" handkerchief to wring and twist in my hands. Even Roger Owens got into the act and wished me a nice day. At first, it was all kind of pleasant. Then I remembered where I was and why—not what I would have chosen for a celebration.

For the next two days, Nan, Roger, Cindy Moisan, and the judge went back and forth—out of hearing of the jury, for most of it—with the DNA expert witnesses, Hal Deadman and Alice Louise Hill, from the FBI. Ultimately, the entire transcript of the trial would total 719 pages; of that, 329 of them involved the admissibility of the DNA evidence. The key statistic at the heart of all the arguments was that, according to the FBI's statistical data base, and what the testing had shown, there was *only one chance in 2.6 billion that Bobby Lee Smith was not my rapist.*

As Roger Owens was later quoted as saying, "I think when that guy (Deadman) says it's him, as opposed to 2.6 billion other people, that's beyond any legal standard. It excludes everyone else in this hemisphere. . . ."

At that point, Judge Gamble ruled that while the jury would

be allowed to hear Mr. Deadman's and Ms. Hill's testimony, what they would not be allowed to hear was that particular statistic. The argument against it was that it was so overwhelming, it would take the discretion of making an innocent-or-guilty decision out of the hands of the jury.

Except for that long-ago first continuance, when John Wellman had to withdraw from defending Bobby Lee Smith because of the conflict of interest, every other damn continuance had revolved around the DNA, around the FBI's reluctance to be forthcoming with their information, and around Roger Owens and Cynthia Moisan needing to find their own independent experts to run the tests and refute the prosecution's results. But once the judge ruled that the "inflammatory" statistic could not be used, there was no longer any reason for Roger and Cynthia to call their defense experts.

The two expert witnesses for the prosecution testified for hours and hours on DNA in general and these DNA tests in particular. What Hal Deadman finally said about our tests was: "The DNA removed from the vaginal swab matches the DNA from the known blood sample of the defendant . . . the probability of obtaining that result by coincidence or by chance is extremely, extremely small."

Halfway through January 30, just after Hal Deadman completed his testimony, the judge excused everyone for lunch. After that break, there was more testimony from Bobby Lee Smith's probation officer and from the man who owns the beauty parlor where Lisa Smith testified she'd had her hair done the day of the rape. And then, around 2:00, Roger Owens abruptly asked for another break.

Something odd had started happening. Steven told me later that there were huddled conversations with the judge, outside the presence of the jury. Roger looked agitated, even angry, as he conferred with Cynthia Moisan, and then appeared to speak very heatedly to his client. The judge's clerk hurriedly left the courtroom for a few minutes and then came back into the room loaded down with law books. The judge talked to Roger,

Roger talked to Bobby, Bobby talked to the judge, the judge talked to Bobby. Something was up.

"I think he's trying to change his plea," Nan told us.

"What does that mean?" we asked.

"Consent," she said. "The DNA testimony scared him, I think. He's going to say innocent, with consent. That he admits yes, he did it, but that you told him it was OK."

Steven and I just looked at each other. This was the craziest yet.

"Can he do that?" I asked, panic rising in my voice.

"He can try," Nan said. A little line of determination had formed around her mouth. "But I don't think Roger will let it happen. The whole thing would just collapse, after all the testimony the past few days. There would have to be a mistrial declared, because Roger would have to excuse himself, and then Smith would have to get a new defense lawyer, and we'd start all over again." She shook her head. "I just don't think that's going to happen."

At 3:30, the judge reconvened the court. Steven went back to his seat, I went back to pacing in the hallway. A mistrial. Starting all over again. I looked at the windows at the end of the hall, measuring their height from the ground. If I jumped now . . .

As Bobby Lee Smith took the stand, I went again to the door to the courtroom and stood looking through the glass at him. I looked at him for what seemed like long minutes before he began to speak. I didn't blink. I didn't look away. I believed at that minute that I could actually will him to announce to the jury he was guilty. What are you going to say, I thought, as I tried to connect with whatever was going on in his head.

As soon as he sat down, he folded his hands in his lap and started to rock back and forth in his chair. He looked over at the jury, and slowly rocked and rocked as he spoke—it was the same motion I would've used to rock my babies.

He testified just as we had thought he would all along. Nothing had changed. He didn't do it, he said. He wasn't there, he didn't do it. It wasn't true about the rings, it wasn't true about the rape. Roger asked him all the questions, then Nan cross-examined him and asked them all again.

"Isn't it true, Mr. Smith, that as you walked down Boyd Street and got to Grand View College, early in the morning, you saw Nancy Ziegenmeyer parked in her car?"

"That's not true."

"Isn't it true, Mr. Smith, that you put a white rag in her face and pushed her over to the passenger side and drove her car away?"

"No, that's not true."

On and on she went, as Steven sat there listening to every single detail of that morning brought to the jury's attention in the form of a question. And as we'd expected, Bobby Lee Smith denied every single one.

Finally, at the end of his testimony, court was adjourned for the day. Closing arguments would be presented the next morning, and then, after the judge gave his instructions, the case would go to the jury.

I watched closely as the jury left the courtroom and came out into the corridor. They weren't supposed to look at me, and I probably wasn't supposed to look at them. Please, I said to the backs of their heads as they walked down the hall. Please.

The next morning the closing argument for the defense came first. Once again I had to stay outside the courtroom. Once again I had to rely on Steven and Jane to tell me later what went on.

Roger Owens ridiculed all the DNA evidence, arguing against convicting someone on the basis of something that no one can even see. He called DNA "hocus-pocus" and referred to the FBI expert, Hal Deadman, as Mr. Wizard. He told the jury that I had not absolutely identified Bobby Lee Smith when I looked at Ralph Roth's photographs, which raised the question of reasonable doubt. He also brought up the Charles

Stuart case in Boston, telling the jury that this was just one more example of a white person falsely accusing a black man of a crime.

Then Nan made her closing argument for the prosecution. She carefully went over all the details of the DNA evidence. She reminded the jury that although I'd only been half sure of my first photo identification, I had been one hundred percent sure with the second set of photographs. And she reminded them again of the irrefutable fact of the rings. My rings had been stolen by my rapist, and Bobby Lee Smith's wife had ended up with them in her possession.

Then the judge instructed, or charged, the jury. He reminded them that the first-degree kidnapping charges included sexual assault; that they could find Bobby Lee Smith guilty of that, or guilty of one of seven lesser charges, but if they could not find him guilty of any of these charges—without reasonable doubt—then they must find him not guilty. And then he excused them to deliberate.

For a few minutes, Steven and I sat close to each other on the bench out in the hallway. I fingered my grandmother's pearls, which I'd put on that morning for good luck. I knew if I kept it up, I'd probably yank them off the string. But I just couldn't sit still.

I wandered down to Helen Youngs's office and ate some of her candy. Then I walked back toward Steven.

Roger Owens was pacing, too. "I'm glad it's over for you," he said to me. "And I hope it *is* over."

Well, maybe for you, I thought, watching him walk away. This is just another case to you. To me, it's my life.

The jury came back in less than ninety minutes.

Nan and Roger and Cindy were at the attorneys' table. Lisa Davis Smith sat across the room, holding the two littlest boys near her, with Bobby's family next to them.

And I was finally in there, too, sitting on that hard bench, where Steven had been sitting alone, since the very first day. He had his arm around me, holding me close. I couldn't take a breath in and I couldn't get a breath out. The silence in that room was so deep that I was sure everybody could hear the tears rolling off my face and hitting my dress. Bobby Lee Smith stood up to hear the verdict.

"We, the jury, find the defendant, Bobby Lee Smith, guilty of the crime of kidnapping in the first degree."

Steven dug his hand hard into my shoulder, pulling me in tight. We couldn't even look at each other.

Fourteen months, twelve days, ten hours, and forty minutes of our lives had gone by since the morning the car door had opened in that parking lot. No, not gone by. Gone. Lost. And now, finally, it had all come down to this one moment.

I looked over at the jury. Some of them looked back at me. Some were crying. Bobby Lee Smith, still standing, had his head down.

The judge thanked the jury and excused them. They were allowed to leave the courtroom first, and Steven and I left right behind them. Bobby Lee Smith was allowed to stay behind, for a few moments with his wife and children. Lisa was holding on to him, crying.

When we got out into the corridor, it seemed full of people, all talking at once. Helen Youngs hugged me, and a couple of people called out "Congratulations!" It struck me as an odd word to use. I looked around, wanting to find Nan, to thank her. Jane Schorer was taking notes, and David Peterson was taking pictures.

Steven walked me to the end of the hall, where we sat down on a wooden bench. I was still trying to get some air inside my lungs. A minute or two later, Judge Gamble came out of the courtroom and walked over to us. He said, "Mrs. Ziegenmeyer, I hope very much that everything works out for you."

Kellye Carter, the *Register* reporter who'd written the daily stories about the trial, came over to us and asked me how I felt about winning. That sounded as odd to me as "congratulations" did.

"There are no winners here," I said to her. "Everybody

loses, because a conviction doesn't take away a rape. It'll never go away."

Down the hall, a deputy was leading Bobby Lee Smith away, to stay in jail until the sentencing. He was in handcuffs. I realized his little boys had seen that.

"Oh, my God, why didn't he think of his children?" I asked. "Why didn't he think of them?" I was still sobbing as Dee Ann and Steven walked me out to the parking lot.

Again, like all of the other long rides home we'd made after the hearings, the depositions, the days of the trial, we stopped at the Kwik-Shop. Chocolate for me, beer for Steven. But this trip was different. This time, when the children greeted us at the door and asked if it was all over, we would at last be able to tell them yes.

CHAPTER TWENTY

ROGER OWENS: "They quoted one juror saying it was the DNA that convinced him Smith was guilty. Ha. That particular juror was asleep. I discount the DNA, and I discount Nancy's identification, but I can't discount the rings, and if I were the jury, I'd probably have done the same thing they did. Those rings were just too damning.

"Now, if Lisa Davis Smith had said two black guys had given them to her, I might've had some room to move. But two Hispanics? Where the hell did they come from? I don't make up this stuff, I can't tell them what to say. I have to go with what my witnesses give me. So I said to her, 'I guess it's all right with me, Lisa, if you can get up there and say that with a straight face.' So she did, and when I saw the jury leaning forward in their seats, I said to myself, 'That's it, the ball game's over.'

"I know Nancy was afraid I was going to harass her about her life before the rape. But as far as I was concerned, it wasn't relevant. What she did for work, what kind of relationship she and Steve had, none of that mattered to me. I was very conscious of Steve in the courtroom, his anger, his bitterness. I think he took a lot of it harder, in a different way, than Nancy did.

"See, I understand that when there's an actual threat to your family, your instincts and your emotions just take over. My

137

wife and my mother were held at gunpoint once, in our house, while it was being robbed. If I'd have been home that night, I'd have shot the kid. Of course, that's why I don't have guns. . . .

"I know it seemed long and drawn out to Nancy. But now that I'm representing union workers, I often see negligence cases, where somebody's crippled, and it takes years to get through the system, to get food on his table, and nobody gives a shit about that. But put a guy away for the rest of his life? Hey, let's get this done in six minutes.

"I couldn't practice law, I don't think, if Iowa had the death penalty. No one—lawyers on either side of the question, or judges—believes the death penalty is truly a deterrent. Killing people off after they've killed someone else off? Doesn't make sense. People who commit violent crime don't think about the penalties while they're committing that crime, and people who commit more than one are pathological, they don't think about anything when they're committing crimes. The death penalty is attacking the problem when it's already too late, and it's being used as a Band-Aid by politicians who are too lazy or too chickenshit to face the people and explain why we have violent crime in this society.

"And I think the death penalty creates a different set of problems for juries. There's a theory that you really want to get those young jurors. Not me. Give me that older juror who remembers something about the Nazis, or Adlai Stevenson, or World War II, or Vietnam. Then, maybe, we'll have a frame of reference for what really goes on in the world. I go back to my hometown of Newton, Iowa, and they think Daniel Ortega's a relief pitcher for the Cubs.

"When Bobby wanted to change his plea, I knew what had happened. I was mad, and disgusted, but I understood him. He heard all that stuff about the DNA, heard a guy in a suit talking about something he didn't understand—a guy from Washington, D.C.!—and he panicked. I told him I could not go forward with a consent plea—we had just spent a whole year preparing a case that said they had the wrong guy. We'd said over and over to the jury that they had the wrong guy. They would've laughed me out of there, and him, too.

"When I'm working on a case, I take it home with me, in my head. I took Bobby Lee Smith and his family home every night. His mother sat in court with her Bible—she was convinced God would take care of Bobby. When he was acquitted in the first trial, she said, 'There, see? God took care of him.' I guess God was winking in the second trial. . . .

"Once a case is over, though, win or lose, I put it behind me. Next case, please! I learned early on that I had to do that or I wouldn't stay a trial lawyer for very long. Each defendant, each trial, is a new one, and worthy of all your emotions, your full attention.

"But for Nancy Ziegenmeyer and Bobby Smith, there is no next case. This is their only case. And I can't begrudge that, for her, or for him either. Something terrible happened to her, I don't deny that, or the trauma of it. But she had the best victims' services available (now *there's* something that the politicians could fix, for all those places that don't have the resources that Polk County, Iowa, has), and she had a justice system that basically gave her the best it could offer. And she has her freedom, and she'll move forward in it now, with her husband and her children. But Bobby's going to be working on this case for the rest of his life. She should be aware of that."

Nan Horvat: "There is a day-to-day tedium in a trial that attorneys get accustomed to. It's the step-by-step that they train for and learn to accommodate in their own expectations. But given what had happened to Nancy, that tedium was hard for her. We come to the courts, we say, to get justice. But victims are often looking for something else—healing, maybe—and that's not necessarily found in a courtroom, no matter what the outcome of a trial is.

"When we talk about the fourteen months, it really isn't that unusual a time frame, because what we all keep forgetting is there was another case involving Bobby Lee Smith going on during that same time, with another victim, who is not public, who is not as safe and secure in her own life as Nancy, who was perhaps not as convincing to a jury as Nancy was in her testimony.

"And in that case, the rapist didn't cover the victim's face, so she had a chance to get a good look at him. Then she came into court, said, 'That's the guy,' and the jury said, 'Not guilty.' I don't know why. Is it that the public doesn't believe that a woman can come into court all by herself, without any scientific evidence or any other evidence to corroborate her testimony, and point at a man and say, 'That person hurt me'? And isn't that the kind of question that historically has always surrounded rape cases? When it's just you against him, why isn't that sufficient? It would be interesting to do some kind of survey of rape crisis workers; I'll bet the first thing they hear victims say is 'No one is going to believe me.'

"Nancy was worried that her life, her troubles with Steven, would influence a jury. She thought Roger would come at her with all guns blazing. And I, of course, didn't know what Roger would do, because nobody ever does. But when she told me she and Steven weren't still married, I asked: Did you introduce him to me as your husband? Do you sleep with him, live with him, use his name, hold him out as your husband? Hey, to me, under the laws of Iowa, you're married. It simply wasn't an issue in this case, and it never made me one bit nervous. And besides, with the rape shield laws, it probably wouldn't have been admissible anyway. It was just a nonissue.

"Sure, Nancy was a pain once in a while, like when she threatened not to testify. I had to get tough there. I can't afford to be manipulated by my witnesses, or I'd lose control of my cases. I had to let her know that I was running this, not her. But her anger, her frustration, and the way that she let me know about it—it was better than being passive. When I get a passive victim, I not only worry about what kind of witness they're going to be, I worry about what kind of life they're going to have when this is all over. I don't worry about Nancy's life now. She's strong, and directed, she's taken all of this and is focusing it in good ways. I think about Steve . . . if he'd jumped over the rail at Bobby, I believe nobody would've been surprised.

"I think, at least locally, the system might be responding a little to the complaints Nancy raised. Prosecutors—me, at least—are a little different. They're beginning to ask: What's my responsibility here, am I doing enough, keeping witnesses informed enough? And judges are drawing the line on continuances. 'One more and that's it: Fish or cut bait.'

"I try not to brood when I lose a case. I lost the one before Nancy's, after all, and another one before that. And I try not to gloat when I win one. Because I don't learn from the ones I win, but from the ones I lose.

"Knowing that the penalty for this crime was life with no parole wasn't necessarily a factor in the way I prosecuted the case, but it would be different if we had the death penalty. I couldn't execute people. I can send them to jail for a long, long time, no problem. But I've always believed the threat of execution is not a deterrent. Plus, it's hugely expensive to a state to fend off the appeals, and there's no evidence that having it changes a single thing.

"When I was in college, two friends of my sister's were brutally murdered in Colorado. It was the luck of the draw that my sister happened to stay in and study that night and wasn't with them, or she would've been dead, too. Would the death penalty have brought any of those girls back? Would it have healed their families? No. That healing has to come about in some other way. If you want to punish the daylights out of someone, you should literally do that—that is, take away their daylight, their sunlight, their sky, their freedom. I can do that, and I can still sleep at night.

"I learned a lot from all of this. Would I want twenty Nancys? No! Besides, one is all it takes to make the difference. And she's the one."

CHAPTER TWENTY-ONE

FOR DAYS AFTER THE TRIAL I wandered around the house in a fog. All these months, every thought I had about the future had been put on hold. Our lives had revolved around The Case, The Continuances, The Lawyers, The Trial. And now we finally had The Verdict. In another few weeks, we would have The Sentence, although we all knew what that would be: life in prison with no parole.

Jane Schorer and Geneva Overholser told me that the newspaper story was tentatively scheduled for sometime near the end of February. It would be a series, they had decided—there was too much stuff here for a one-day story. In the meantime, there was more reporting to be done, more pictures to be taken, the writing, the editing. I was, as I was about mostly everything lately, ambivalent. Yes, I wanted to see the story in print. No, I didn't want to see the story in print.

In the meantime, Steven went back to work, with a loud and fervent wish that now this family would please return to normal, or whatever normal was for us. It was time to pick up the fragments of our lives and begin to put them back together—that is, the ones that could be put back together. I had learned that some of what had happened could never be mended, the scars would always be there. But I was determined to piece back together what I could. And I had to set my feet in some new direction, even though it wasn't yet clear to me what that direction should be.

The first thing I did was get sick. There are a couple of interpretations for this, I guess. Either it was nature's way of telling me to lie down and shut up, or it was the result of all the poison I'd been accumulating since November 1988. I had one of those colds that goes into your head, your nose, your chest, your back—everywhere, right down to your feet. For days I stayed in bed, in my old gray sweatshirt, drinking juice and Coke, eating chocolate, watching "Guiding Light," and feeling miserable. But it was a nice kind of miserable—not quite like taking a vacation but more comfortable, somehow, than I'd been in months. When it was all over, I felt as if my batteries had been recharged. A good thing, too, because there were still battles left to fight.

For one, we were still getting the bill from Mercy Hospital for the medical attention I'd received the morning of the rape. The hospital had turned it over to a collection agency in Iowa City, and the agency was calling me, it seemed, almost daily. I angrily told them that the man who raped me was in Polk County Jail, and I gave them Bobby Lee Smith's name. "Send the damn bill to him," I said.

But after more phone calls, including one to Bill Olson, I decided I would have to handle it myself. I drove to Des Moines, straight to the Iowa Department of Health's office. I walked in there with the bill in my hand, told them who I was, and said, "I don't pay this bill. You do." And I walked out. That was the last we heard of it.

The dream I'd had months before about going to work for the attorney general still stuck with me, so one day I just picked up the telephone and called Tom Miller's office. I want to do something about victims' rights, I told him. I want to take what I've learned and put it to work somehow, maybe turn it into something positive, for me, and for somebody else.

He invited me to come to his office, and I did. We talked a long time that day, about victimization, victims' rights, the role that legislators play, and the role for an ordinary citizen. He sent me home with much to think about.

•

One day we received a check in the mail. It was from the Polk County Courthouse—my compensation check for going to Des Moines to testify in Case Number 41733, *State of Iowa* vs. *Bobby Lee Smith*. Someone told me later that this case had cost the state approximately $200,000, maybe even more. My pay for being a witness (and this includes mileage) was $33.10. That'll go a long way at Wally World, I thought.

As life slowly began to return to normal, I carried on with the usual, day-to-day responsibilities of any wife and mother. I had a husband and three active children. Piano lessons, and dance lessons, and PTA. In spring, there would be Little League for the boys and Sissy's dance recital. In the meantime, three meals a day to fix (Steven has always come home for lunch), and laundry, and cleaning house. Family birthdays, and anniversaries, and bowling on Friday nights. All these things had sustained me throughout the past months. But now, maybe I could begin to find some joy in them, where for so long there had been none.

Oh, I still had my nightmares, and the fear of crowds. A car backfiring or an unexpected knock at the door when I was home alone could still make me nauseated with quick fear. But it was beginning to be a little easier to shake it off.

Jane told me that the newspaper series would begin in the February 25 edition of the *Des Moines Register*—a Sunday. For months I had shared some of my deepest fears and memories with her, and the closer it got to the publication date, the more nervous I was. How would it read? What would people think?

I had some errands to run and shopping to do in the city the week before, so I thought that as long as I was there, I'd just run into the paper and read whatever they'd put together at that point. When Geneva came out of her office, she smiled and asked me to come in.

When I told her why I'd come, she got this funny look on her face.

"Nancy," she said, "I'm afraid we can't let you see the copy for the series. It's our policy not to let anyone read stories before they're actually published in the paper."

I couldn't believe what I'd heard.

"But Geneva," I protested, "this is different, isn't it? I mean, this isn't like a normal news story, like a city council meeting, or a car crash or something. It's about me, and the most private parts of my life. What if there's something in there that I don't like? What if there's something in there that's just plain old wrong? Of course I'm entitled to see it. Aren't I?"

But no, she assured me, I wasn't. It had never been the *Register's* policy to let a news source see or make any changes in copy in advance of publication. So that's what I've become, I thought. First a victim, then a survivor, then a witness, and now, a news source. Why was I always the last one to get the word about these changing roles I kept getting stuck in?

She was sorry, Geneva continued, and she certainly understood how I felt, given the nature of the story and all, but she just didn't feel she could make an exception in this case.

I begged, I pleaded, I did everything but grovel. I simply couldn't believe that I didn't have access to something I basically saw as mine. My life, my family, my rape. How could the story not be mine? After all, I had come to the paper, I had cooperated with Jane and David, there was little or nothing they didn't know now about our lives—and yet I couldn't get in there and change so much as a comma.

Jane and I had been working together for almost seven months. There had been more than fifty phone calls and visits, endless hours of going over detail after detail. We'd cried together, I'd told her some of my most secret things, and she in turn had shared with me a lot of private information about her life. I had trusted her, and trusted Geneva, and not once during all that time did anyone say one single word or give me the smallest hint that I would have no control whatsoever over the finished product. I'd have to read it on Sunday, just like anybody else in Iowa, and that was all there was to it.

But I just assumed. . . . And right there was where I'd made my mistake. Steven has a saying about the word *assume*: Break down the spelling, it makes an ass of u and me. Once again, somebody else was in charge of my life. I couldn't believe I hadn't seen it coming.

In my car, I have a cassette tape of an old Meat Loaf album from the seventies, *Bat Out of Hell*. I've come to think of it as stress therapy—there are some songs on that tape that would shatter glass. All the way back to Grinnell, I played that tape just as loud as I could crank it, and went through half a pack of cigarettes. I guess it's some kind of tribute to modern automotive engineering that all the car windows were still in place when I turned into the driveway.

By Sunday I was a totally crazy woman. Months later someone told me that Geneva had said, "If Nancy had known where the printing plant was, she'd have gone there in the middle of the night, sat down at the front gate, and waited for the first copy to roll off the presses." Too bad I didn't think of that at the time. When Steven came through the front door with the paper, I snatched it out of his hands and threw it on the kitchen table.

There it was. "It Couldn't Happen to Me: One Woman's Story."

The children walked over to the table and took a look. Nick and Sissy didn't say anything, but Benjamin looked at the paper, then looked up at me, then looked back at the paper again. "Mom, Mom," he whispered, his brown eyes opened wide in surprise, "you're on the front page of the paper!"

For the next five days, we lived from one day's newspaper to the next. Each day there was a new segment of the series, and each segment brought back memories and details that still had enormous power, power to anger, sadden, and surprise us. There were pictures of me with Dee Ann, me at the bowling alley, me and Nan Horvat in the courtroom, Bobby Lee Smith standing alone in court the day of the verdict.

I had heard a couple of details from Jane about various decisions Geneva had made concerning the series: the way the rape itself would be represented, the details, the graphic language. But the word *penis* jumped right out at me, and so did the word *vagina*. They were certainly words I used, but I couldn't remember ever seeing them in the newspaper before. And I was surprised to see myself called "Ziegenmeyer" throughout the whole series. It seemed so cold and distant, in the middle of all these other intimate details. On the other hand, I reminded myself, news sources get called by their last names.

Now that it was real, we braced ourselves for the hate mail we'd get, the friendships we might lose, the relatives who would wish they weren't related. My mother would probably have to deal with a lot of garbage from her friends. Steven would probably have to put up with the same kind of garbage at work. But to our complete surprise, that's not what happened.

After the first day, the phone started to ring. I began to hear from people who, although they knew either me or Steven, were hearing the story for the first time. They were kind, and concerned with how we were now, how we had gotten through it all.

Within four or five days, the mail started to come. At first it was notes from people I'd known: people I'd gone to school with, a teacher from grade school, friends who had moved away from Grinnell. Then came the ones from people I didn't know, who knew me only through what they read in the paper. Women, mostly, but men, too. I would quickly read through them, looking for the accusations, the condemnation, the question: What kind of woman goes public with this kind of story? But all I saw were kind words, comforting words. Letter after letter was full of only positive things to say to me, and to my husband, about what these people were reading in their newspapers.

And in a few more days, I started seeing another kind of

letter: the ones from victims. Women who'd been raped last year, two years ago, five years ago, ten years ago, forty years ago. Women who had been raped when they were children, or raped by their boyfriends in college, or raped by men who climbed into windows and held guns to their heads, or raped by estranged husbands who "had their rights." Women who had never told anyone, not even their husbands, or their doctors, or their mothers, or their ministers. Women who'd lived in silence with their secret, and had believed they were alone, and somehow to blame. Every day, more phone calls, more letters, from farther and farther away. They were all out there someplace, and they were all talking to me.

It was simply the most amazing thing I had ever seen.

CHAPTER TWENTY-TWO

DEAR NANCY ZIEGENMEYER:

"I work in a woman's shelter, and we've had several cases turn out very badly lately. I can't tell you how much it meant to our residents to know that someone has prevailed. We cried as well as rejoiced for you."

"I read your story, and looked at the pictures, and there was something so familiar about you. And then it came to me: it was my little fourth-grade girl, sitting to my left in the front row. I remember your bubbly disposition. I am so proud to have been your teacher."

"You have been on my mind because my only daughter was raped by someone she knew. When the detectives interviewed her, they said she didn't have a case. You and Steven have the love and fortitude we all envy."

"My daughter and I read your series together. She is a college student, and is angry that campus rape is treated so lightly. She told me how several friends were raped, and never reported it out of fear. We were able to discuss this openly, and maybe educate ourselves."

•

"I am a sixty-year-old farmer. I write out of deep gratitude for you. Your witness counts for more to me than that of any other Iowan I've known."

"Some months ago, my lovely sixteen-year-old daughter was kidnapped, tied up, and sexually assaulted. She was able to press charges but did not want to go to trial. None of us felt that she could succeed in her daily life at school if her peers found out. We are deeply moved by the amount of courage *BOTH* of you have displayed."

"When I was fifteen, I was raped. I can still hear my rapist laugh. To add to the emotional pain, I was wearing a tampon at the time, and he did not let me remove it. The physical pain was excruciating. I only spoke of this once, to a friend. Her response was, 'How can you live with yourself?' I never told anyone again. It has been nine years. I have never had a boyfriend, or made love. I wish I could be part of a strong sisterhood of survivors. I hope you are that first link in the chain of recovery. Rape victims never have a name or a face. You are helping me find mine."

"My husband had abused me for years. After leaving him, I found out that he had also abused our daughters, ages two and six. We were fortunate to find an excellent therapist, but the legal system was less than sympathetic. I had to wage a war to get anything done. Our county attorney had never prosecuted such a case, and kept putting me off. We finally got my husband on one count, but not on the second, because my youngest daughter was unable to give testimony. I will always feel I failed her. I commend you for your courage, and your example."

"As a child, I was the victim of sexual abuse. Through my husband and children, I found the strength to enter therapy. Now I am whole, but never will I be the same. The love of others will be given to you tenfold, for the part of yourself you are giving to all victims."

"Forty years ago, I was the victim of childhood sexual abuse. I still sleep with a gun under my pillow, get up in the middle of the night to check every noise, and to make sure doors are locked. I thank you for the courage you displayed. That's the type of courage a half-breed, ex-fighter can't seem to find. But keep speaking out, perhaps some other person, alone, without the support of a lifemate, needs to hear your words."

"I am a thirty-seven-year-old black male on Georgia's death row. I am deeply saddened to learn of the terrible act of violence that was inflicted on you, and I want to commend you for having the courage to speak out. Maybe others will follow suit, and cause a change in the way society treats rape victims."

"I am a fifty-two-year-old married man, with two girls in college. I love my wife of twenty-seven years very much. Ten weeks before we were to be married, she was abducted by a convict, two months out of prison, and raped at gunpoint. I still harbor a burning rage against the rapist and an indifferent legal system. Your courage is to be commended. I wish we had the same strength."

"I was raped two years ago. I, like you, have children. I tried to tell my husband, the police, my friends, but couldn't quite do it. It took three months to admit to my therapist, and then my husband, that I was raped. It took a year and a half of counseling and the gentle understanding of my husband to feel confident and safe again. But it still hurts, and I still cry."

"I have been a police officer for fifteen years. Although I have always attempted to handle sexual assault victims with compassion, your story has given me new insight. I intend to make it available to our Sexual Assault Investigations Detail. I think every detective could learn from your story."

"I am the survivor of childhood incest. You are an inspiration to me, because after thirty-five years of silence, I finally came forward to seek help for the trauma that is still with me at age fifty."

"It has been a year since I was kidnapped, terrorized, and repeatedly raped. A year of pure hell. I didn't tell anyone for six weeks. My friends said, 'Just forget about it, you're alive, you're lucky he didn't kill you. You'll get over it.' But he did murder me—he murdered my soul."

"My two sisters were raped back in the mid-fifties, when they were only eleven and thirteen, and it changed them and our family. Their attackers were never caught, and their innocence was stripped from them forever. I wish you God's speed in your healing."

"It will soon be twelve years since I was date raped, at gunpoint. Because I had been to bed with this man once before, I was ashamed to report the crime. I felt like I was the bad person. From time to time, I wonder how many other women have been victimized by him, because of my not reporting it. None, I hope, but I fear many."

"I was a victim twice, once when I was fifteen, a second time a year later. This happened in the 1960s. I finally shared my experience—only with my family—four years ago. God bless you, and give you peace."

"I was raped two weeks after I started college. I reported the rape to the college police. They told me to think about it for a week, and come back if I still wanted to press charges. By then, all I wanted to do was forget it. It took me two years to get professional help. I help at a rape crisis center now. Thank you from all of the women you've helped, and will help."

"I was raped when I was nine by a stranger in my neighborhood. I am sick of this bullshit that we have to survive in silence. My roommate recently told me she was date raped when she was a teenager—I'm the first person she ever told. I am sick of standing in the darkness with my pain, and I want this to stop. I will be damned if I let it continue unabated without my scream of protest."

"We were more fortunate than many, because our fifteen-year-old daughter revealed to us what happened to her. The perpetrator was someone she cared about, and he threatened suicide if she told. There was no way a physical exam could substantiate the rape, and her word of what happened means nothing to the county attorney. What can we do to help to change our laws, so that our daughter and others can be 'rape survivors' instead of victims?"

"Although I am not a victim, I'm still victimized by this crime, because I'm afraid to go anywhere. I fear for my daughter, for the days when she will be independent, and I won't be able to protect her. Thank you for your courage."

This is only a small sample of the voices we heard in those first few days. Of them all, there was one that was especially dear:

"I am amazed and pleased that you've been able to tell your story. I am sure you will receive some victims' rights awards, and the *Register* some literary awards. And I know you will and have helped other victims cope with what they've gone through. Love, Dad."

CHAPTER TWENTY-THREE

Geneva Overholser: "I pride myself on being a consensus builder, and I didn't want anybody around the paper to feel like I rammed this story down anybody's throat. So at one point in the editing process, in order to respond to everybody's concerns, I assembled the city editor, the Sunday editor, the features editor who was working with Jane Schorer, and my deputy managing editor, and said, OK, let's deal with all of these issues. And we sat around a table and began to cut through what we saw as some of the sticking points in the series.

"For instance, my view from the beginning was that whatever Nancy Ziegenmeyer was or was not, we didn't need her to be either chaste and virginal, or sluttish and wanton. She didn't need to be any kind of ideal woman. One of society's perceptual errors in dealing with rape, and we all know this, is either that the victim asked for it, or it doesn't happen to nice girls. The point is really about choice. In our lives, we mostly have choices about our actions. But a victim doesn't have any choice in what happens to her in those moments when she's being raped, and who or what she's done or been before doesn't matter.

"However, the fact that Nancy and Steve were no longer married at that point did raise a small red flag with me. Nan Horvat had decided that according to the laws of the state of

Iowa, they were common-law man and wife, and that's the way it would be dealt with in court. But we decided not to refer to them in the series specifically as husband and wife. We allowed them to be presented in the way they present themselves: in a life and a home they share together, with their children, in a community that recognizes them as a family. I wanted very much to be absolutely accurate, but I didn't want to throw in a bunch of stuff about their marital history that was going to color the way people felt about her. The question then becomes, I guess, 'strictly speaking,' is she married? I wasn't interested in hiding the fact that she wasn't, I just didn't want to get into a three- or four-paragraph explanation of all of that, like 'Well, they used to be married, and then they got a divorce, and now they're back together, etc., etc.' Still, journalists must deal all the time with 'strictly speaking.' . . . It was a bit of a tough call, and I suppose it can be argued either way.

"Another decision we had to make was what to call her. Jane had called her 'Nancy' throughout, because she was closer to her. But somebody suggested that it sounded as if we were condescending to her, that the use of the familiar somehow diminished her. After all, we didn't call Smith 'Bobby' or 'Bobby Lee.' So I made the choice of what I think of as the more formal 'Ziegenmeyer,' because although the overall style of the piece was softer than what the *Register* would normally have printed, I wanted it to carry some kind of newspaper weight. Using only her last name seemed to add that weight, and gave us a way to look at her with some objectivity.

"Then we hassled quite a bit on how to describe the rape itself. I felt very strongly that we needed to hold to the power of it, and the plain, clear language does that. There's not a word in the description that we hadn't used before in this paper. We've used penis, we've used anal intercourse. We took out some details that seemed unnecessary; for instance, there were various pants going up and down more times than they needed to.

"One large consideration, of course, was race. We couldn't take race out of the issue, because Smith himself had injected race as an issue. But we didn't need to keep referring to him as a black man every time he did something or said something. So we referred to it where it was appropriate, and cut it where it wasn't. And I tried to address this in my comments that accompanied the first day's article, with the statistics I cited; that this case was an anomaly, and that only 4 percent of rapes reported nationally involve a black man and a white woman.

"We cut back on the DNA a little, because while it was important to the continuances, it turned out not to be as instrumental in the verdict as we thought it would be.

"The night before we ran the first story, Saturday night, I stayed late at the paper, monitoring the editing process on my computer terminal. I was a little anxious—I was uncharacteristically close to this one, so I was shepherding it through.

"From the very beginning, when the piece first came in, I had seen a tendency to change things here and there, a word, a phrase. Body parts, for instance. Every once in a while, somebody would come across something that made them wince.

"So that night, all of a sudden, I see on my screen that somebody's changed 'after he ejaculated' to 'when he had finished.' So I sent a message on my terminal: CHANGE THIS BACK. Then I went down into the newsroom, thinking they must be wondering what was going on. I mean, I don't usually sit here grandly sending electronic messages to the copy editors.

"I explained that this was a series I cared a lot about, and I wanted us to do it right, and hoped that everyone felt the same way I did. And one of the editors said, yes, he did understand. And then he said, 'Oh, besides that, I want you to know my sister was raped, and I've never really been able to deal with her about it. This series is going to help.' I was stunned, because just that afternoon, I'd checked with the deputy editor who would be on the desk on Sunday afternoon, the day the story would come out, just to make sure he was prepared for whatever phone calls or reaction he might get. I asked him if he was going to feel comfortable responding to the callers, and he said yes, and then he said, 'I want you to know that I have a really good friend who was raped, and I've never really been able to talk to her about it, and this is really going to help.' Two people, in my own newsroom, on the same day! It was the first real sense I had of the real impact the series would have, and the audience that was out there for it.

"The response was amazingly positive, positive about Nancy, with a lot of pride in having an Iowan who was that forthright and brave, and positive about us, the paper, that it was the right thing for us to do. There was a whole lot of feeling that the time had come for this issue. Letters poured in endlessly, saying, 'I was raped and I can't talk to anybody about it, and this has saved me from oblivion.'

"That's what my advocacy for openness has been about: not just about being a battering ram for invasion-of-privacy issues, which is the way some people have seen it, but knowing that for a lot of women, this would be a release of pain. You know, when you've been mugged, or your house has been broken into, you want to talk about it endlessly. You want to say, 'Can you believe this, can you believe this?' And here is a crime more horrible than any other, except murder, maybe, but people aren't supposed to talk about it. That's a doubling of the crime. It kicks the victim twice.

"As a culture, we're very strange about anything having to do with sexuality, or anything that's perceived as sexual. We react with a weird combination of puritanism and absolute lasciviousness. The lasciviousness comes out of the puritan thing, we all know that, and we grapple with it. And this story was part of breaking some of that down, because the rape was neither puritanical or lascivious. It was a crime.

"The response in the first days after the series ran quickly became frenzied. The phone messages started stacking up, and the letters, and then, gradually, the media craziness. Other newspapers, the weekly newsmagazines, the networks, and radio, and then all this talk about movies and books. I gave hundreds of interviews in the beginning, but finally had to start turning things down. It gave rise to a lot of examination on our part here. I mean, what is the exact role of a newspaper after a story like this takes on the kind of national prominence this did? Do we all become movie stars? Does the newsroom become a set? Do we all rush out and get agents, and go on 'Donahue'? Was this what we wanted? No.

"And the media got strange about the fact that it happened in Iowa. It's what happens around here during the presidential caucuses. 'Here's a real cow,' or 'Here's a real farmer.' *Time*, or *Newsweek*, I can't remember which, said something like 'even in pastoral Iowa' in this 'Believe It or Not' kind of approach. Raped in pastoral Iowa! It was patronizing, and ignorant, and provincial. People in Iowa know full well that crime happens here. And the story itself made all the more powerful the very point that it can happen, does happen, to anyone, anywhere. And in fact, that's what the statistics have been telling us all along.

"One mistake I want desperately to correct, and that's about something that showed up a week or two later in the *New York Times* piece about the series. I had told the *Times* reporter that one of my editors said that 'Mothers of twelve-year-olds, and blue-haired ladies, will be offended by this series.' The way it got printed, on the front page no less, is that *I* was the one who said it, not that I was quoting someone *else* saying it. First, I never would have said 'blue-haired ladies,' and second, I *am* the mother of a twelve-year-old. I was totally mortified. Even my brother called and said, 'Did you really say that?' And besides, I always thought it might be the *fathers* of twelve-year-olds, and balding men, who would be offended. . . . In fact, it was the alleged blue-haired ladies who wrote in and told us it was about time we did something like this.

"This series wasn't one of those big songs that we and other papers put together, where you assign reporters for a year, and make a big push, and hope for prizes. We just did it because we knew it was the right thing to do. It did good, for our readers, for society. I've never ceased to be both admiring and grateful to Nancy, because it made one hell of a story."

CHAPTER TWENTY-FOUR

THE SAME AMOUNT OF MAIL that was coming to me was also being delivered to the *Des Moines Register*. And within a few days after the last piece in the series ran, Geneva was contacted by newspapers, radio stations, and TV reporters from all over the country.

They wanted to come to Iowa to talk to Geneva and Jane, and they wanted to come to Grinnell, to talk to me. There were requests for long interviews, short interviews, phone interviews, fax interviews. They wanted to ask me more questions. What more could anybody possibly want to know, I wondered, completely amazed as one by one, each of the TV networks called from New York.

I was invited to be on "CBS This Morning" and "NBC Nightly News," and ABC's "Good Morning America" and "Nightline." There was an op-ed piece about Geneva and the series in the *Wall Street Journal*. On March 22, the *Des Moines Register* series was reprinted in England. On March 25, there was a story on the front page of the Sunday *New York Times*. On March 28, the *International Herald Tribune*—in Paris!—reprinted the *New York Times* piece. *Time* magazine called. Within a couple of weeks, I even received a letter from a man in Durban, South Africa, with a copy of a column about the series that had run in his local newspaper.

We had to get call-waiting for the phone, and an answering

machine. I was fast losing ground with answering the mail, and Bill Olson's law office had begun to resemble a travel agency as I got booked on one television news or talk show after another. Steven, never one to waste words, said it all.

"This is getting pretty fucking crazy!"

Early one morning I left Grinnell and drove into Des Moines to witness Bobby Lee Smith's sentencing. From there, I was to fly to New York City to be on "CBS This Morning" the next day. Steven, who doesn't like to fly, thought it was better that he stay in Grinnell with the children, so I had asked Cathy Burnham to make the trip with me. We'd stay overnight in a hotel, and then fly back to Iowa late the following after noon.

The uproar of the past weeks had completely frazzled me—I felt a little like Dorothy in *The Wizard of Oz* the day the tornado flung her house around the skies over Kansas. I'm really just like anybody else: I almost always watch the news on TV, and I try to pay attention to what I see and hear there. To have it so quickly reversed, to think of people paying that kind of attention to me . . . But I was looking forward to the trip. The only traveling I'd done in more than a year was the long, grinding stretch of Interstate 80 from Grinnell to Des Moines and back again. And I'd never been East at all. It wouldn't be a vacation, but once the sentencing was over, it would be a good way to begin to put the bad times behind me.

Cathy and I met Dee Ann Wolfe at the courthouse, in the hallway right outside Judge Gamble's courtroom. Sitting on the hard wooden benches I'd sat on all during the trial, we quietly waited for the doors to open. Even though I knew what was coming, even though I knew this was the last time I'd have to face him, I was still more than a little scared.

The day before the sentencing, the *Register* had run a follow-up piece on the case, and Bobby Lee Smith and Lisa Smith were both quoted as saying the arrest, charges, and verdict all happened only because they were both black.

I guess I had known something like this was inevitable, but I still hated to see it in print.

"I still believe in this country we have a lot of racism," said Smith. "They feel that blacks are more violent, so we're going to put them away. Society has accepted that."

It was hard to deny some of what he was saying. There is racism in this society, and people do have knee-jerk reactions to the complicated issues tangled up with crime and race. And I couldn't deny that, ever since the rape, if a black man came down the aisle toward me at Wal-Mart, I would freeze until he'd gone past. I had never been afraid of black people before in my whole life. I didn't want to be afraid now. But the fear had become as much a part of me as my arms and legs were, and I simply didn't know what to do about that.

The piece in the paper made me wish there had been black people on the jury, that the one black alternate wasn't enough. It wouldn't have changed what was true, and I don't believe it would have changed the jury's decision, but maybe it would have taken the sting out of the accusation that this trial and this verdict were somehow all about race. This crime was not about race, I kept repeating over and over, any more than it was about sex. It was violence.

When we walked into the courtroom, we were all surprised to see Bobby Lee Smith's sons there, along with the rest of his family. The oldest was barely twelve. They're just babies, I thought to myself. Why do these children have to listen to this? Why do they have to see him in handcuffs, brought into the room by a uniformed officer with a gun? Only later did I find out that, except for the once-a-month visits, this would be the last time they would spend any time with their father. He would be going directly from the courtroom to prison.

According to the transcript, it took exactly five minutes, from 8:50 to 8:55.

"Kidnapping in the first degree is a Class A felony," said Judge Gamble. "Pursuant to Iowa Code Section 902.1, the Court has no discretion in connection with the sentencing.

Mr. Smith, you are committed to the custody of the Director of the Department of Adult Corrections for a term of life in prison. Let the record show that the Court has considered the nature of the crime and the impact it has had on the victim. This sentence will provide the defendant with the maximum opportunity for rehabilitation, while protecting the community from further crimes by this defendant, and the Court hopes that this sentence will serve to deter others from similar criminal activity in the future."

I knew, when I walked into the courtroom that morning, that in spite of the fear I felt, there was nothing there that could hurt me anymore. There was nothing the system could do, nothing Roger Owens could do, nothing Bobby Lee Smith could do.

But I wasn't prepared for what the faces of his children did. Their eyes looked as the eyes of my own children had looked so often over the past months: big, and sad, and questioning, and frightened of what the grown-ups could not explain away.

In my head, I heard again the frightening words from that November morning. He wouldn't kill me, he said, because he knew what it was like to grow up with only one parent. Crying one more time, I held on tight to my friends, and knew that I wasn't the only victim in that room.

It was a bright spring day, and as the plane circled New York in preparation for landing, Cathy and I looked through the windows, to the city beneath us. So many buildings, as far as we could see. Two rivers, and a sliver of shiny ocean, and the Statue of Liberty. The Empire State Building! The World Trade Center! And so much sunshine we couldn't look without squinting.

CBS had promised that a car would pick us up and take us into Manhattan. The driver has the flight number, and he'll get to the airport in plenty of time, they said. He'll be holding a big sign with your name on it, they said. No problem.

So we got off the plane, and we looked, and we waited, and

we looked some more. Lots of people, lots of noise, lots of construction. No man, no sign. Toto, I said to myself, I don't think we're in Kansas anymore.

We wandered around until we found a pay phone, me thinking that any minute we'd be grabbed, kidnapped, and killed. Neither Cathy nor I had the first clue about where we were going, or how to get there, and there was no way I was going to go out on that street by myself and find a taxicab.

With sweaty hands, I looked up the number they'd given me. "Where's our car?" I asked when they answered the phone. My voice was shaking. I was a long damn way from home, a long way from my Steven. In all the months, this was the first time I had been without him, and I didn't like the way it felt. I thought I could probably handle it, but I wasn't sure I wanted to.

The driver finally arrived nearly an hour later. By then, Cathy and I were both ready to jump out of our skin.

We rode into Manhattan with our noses pressed to the car windows. The city looked bigger and noisier and scarier than it had from the air. And I had never seen traffic like this. Where were all these people going?

We arrived at our hotel, the Parker Meridien, at around 6:00 P.M. As we walked through the lobby, I felt like a little kid only pretending to be a grown-up. Everything here was so elegant, I clutched Cathy's arm until we got safely into our room and she'd locked the door behind us.

That night, we only went as far as downstairs to the hotel restaurant for dinner. I knew the great big city was just outside, but I would need daylight and steadier nerves before I could go out and take a closer look at it.

The next morning, a car sent by CBS picked us up at around 7:30 and took us to the studio. I'd had only coffee and a cigarette for breakfast—there was no way I could've swallowed actual food. During the ride, and during the whole time I was sitting in the chair while somebody did my makeup, I kept thinking, "I don't believe this, I don't believe this."

Harry Smith was the one who interviewed me. He sounded

so much like guys I'd grown up with, I decided he must be from the Midwest. He looked right into my eyes as we talked, mostly about the aftermath of the rape, and why I'd gone to Geneva at the paper, and how I hoped this would somehow help other women. It was all over in minutes, and I couldn't even remember what I'd said.

Our flight back didn't leave until late that afternoon, so Cathy and I ventured out to walk up Fifth Avenue. It was the most beautiful spring day, and it was hard to decide whether to look in the windows or stare at the people walking along the sidewalk. Every once in a while someone would bump into me, or crowd past me, and I'd flinch, and grab Cathy's arm.

We went into Saks Fifth Avenue, and came right back out again, dazzled but with all our money intact. "It's not Wal-Mart," we laughed.

We walked slowly up the street, past St. Patrick's Cathedral, looking up at the tall steeple. When we got into Trump Tower, I felt my jaw drop. "My God, who polishes all this brass?" I wondered. And why on earth would anyone ever have put a waterfall inside a building?

After we'd stared into every glass display counter on the first floor of Tiffany's, and spent hundreds of imaginary dollars, we went back out into the bright sunshine. "Let's walk into the park," Cathy suggested.

"What park?" I asked.

"Central Park," she said. "That's it, right up there."

I froze. "No," I said.

"Nancy, it's broad daylight. There's lots of people there, probably cops everyplace. It's supposed to be really beautiful. Somebody at the hotel this morning said the tulips were up."

"No," was all I could manage. Not me, not into that park, not even for tulips. I'd been keeping up with the story of the jogger—she was out of the hospital, she'd gone back to work, they were going to begin picking a jury for the first trial soon. Maybe someday, after all the verdicts were in, maybe then I could go into Central Park. But not now, not yet.

CHAPTER TWENTY-FIVE

ONE AFTERNOON near the end of March, Bill Olson accompanied me to New York so that I could be on ABC's "Good Morning America," with Joan Lunden, early the next morning. After the interview, we planned to jump right back on the plane and head home to Iowa.

We were practically on our way when ABC let us know that they wanted me on "Nightline," with Forrest Sawyer as host, that very same night. It was too late to change plans and planes and stay in New York, so it was decided that I would go to the studio in Ames, Iowa, and be bounced by satellite to New York.

When Bill and I landed in Des Moines, ABC's limo met us at the airport and drove us the thirty-five miles to Ames. It had been a long day, and I was completely out of steam. The weather reflected my mood—it had turned cold and rainy, and I hadn't brought a coat with me. Bill, who is well over six feet tall, loaned me his oversize trench coat; half asleep in the back of the car, I must've looked like a vagrant. I reminded myself of nothing so much as Sissy in one of her worst be-very-careful-I'm-going-to-pitch-a-fit-in-a-minute moods.

I had wanted attention to be paid to the issue of sexual violence, and to what the victim of it has to go through. Now people were paying attention. My wish had come true, and it was like riding a runaway horse. I didn't want to complain, but

I would have liked to grab hold of the reins and slow things down just a bit.

I sat alone in the studio in Ames, hooked up to microphones and cameras, and tried to talk intelligently to people I couldn't see. Bill was in the control room, watching all the monitors.

The topic for discussion that night was "Protecting Rape Victims' Identities: Helping or Hurting?" There were other people on the program: a social worker from Boston, Victoria Ryback, who counsels rape victims, and New York Times columnist Anna Quindlen. In addition, they had taped segments from newspaper people: Jerry Nachman of the New York Post and Wilbert Tatum, the publisher and editor of the Amsterdam News, who had actually printed the Central Park jogger's name in the early days of the press coverage. And there was feminist author Susan Brownmiller, who agreed with Geneva Overholser's stance: that publicizing a victim's name—treating this crime like other crimes—would desexualize the crime and maybe even give us more convictions.

When it was my turn, I tried to stress that I didn't go public until I'd had plenty of time for healing, and that I strongly felt that the name of a victim should never be published without the victim's permission. I also told Forrest Sawyer that while the response to the newspaper series itself had been very positive, people still didn't quite know what to do with me. I compared it to having had a death in the family: Nobody knows quite what to say, and so they're always afraid of saying the wrong thing. Unwanted publicity, and the scrutiny it would bring, could only make that kind of tension worse for a victim, not better. And if a victim believed she was going to end up reading her name in the paper before she was prepared for that, maybe that would be just one more reason not to report the crime at all.

Near the end of the program, Sawyer, after warning me that we had only about thirty seconds remaining, asked about the misconceptions about rape victims that I was still hearing.

At that point, his question registered as a complicated one, and I was fresh out of easy answers. I had to stop and think for a moment, and that ate up most of the remaining time. Just as I was in clumsy midsentence, he cut me off.

"Ms. Ziegenmeyer, I'm sorry to say we're out of time. I think we understood what you were trying to say there." And then he thanked me for coming, and then, I thought, the satellite feed to New York had ended.

I got mad. Mad at myself for answering slowly, mad at Forrest Sawyer for cutting me off. Without thinking, I flipped him the finger.

In the control room, Bill Olson, sitting there watching all twelve monitors, saw what I did. And in New York, Forrest Sawyer saw me, too. The rest of the country, thank God, did not.

On April 3, I flew back to New York again, this time with Jean Pendleton, a partner in Bill Olson's law firm. She's the one who had been working with Bill on the research necessary to press the premises liability matter with Grand View College, and I'd gone over the details of that morning with her almost as often as I had done with Bill.

Jeannie P., as I call her, is a former high school English teacher and a dear friend. Not only does she occasionally correct my grammar, but she also lets me ride her horses and tries to help me mind my manners. Like Bill and Steven, she never lets me forget the value of common sense. For instance, on this day we were flying on Northwest, the first airline to impose the no-smoking rule, and Jeannie strongly suggested that this might be a good way to kick my cigarette habit.

Ever since the incident on "Nightline," I'd realized that I had to learn to deal with the stress of the many ways my life was changing. I wanted to be an advocate for victims in the hope that my story would somehow help others. Now that the opportunities were presenting themselves, I couldn't just flip the finger or run off at the mouth every time the tension built up, not if I wanted to be taken seriously.

And I did want to be taken seriously. What I had learned,

what I had to say, was too important to me. But I had to find a safe middle ground, a way to combine some dignity with a sense of humor. And maybe it was about time to start enjoying some of the excitement. A good place to begin was this trip. I was going to be on "Donahue"!

Phil Donahue has always been one of my heroes. As any mother knows, staying at home with small children can reduce a grown woman to a babbling idiot who can't manage a sentence with more than three words in it. Watching his show every day always helped me remember I was a halfway intelligent adult. I used to come away from it feeling like maybe I'd learned something.

Oh, sure, there are the shows everybody makes fun of, the ones with left-handed bisexuals who raise circus animals, or grandmothers whose sons cry too much, or some other silly thing. But those are the exception to the rule, at least from the living room where I've been sitting.

I've learned about breast cancer, about disciplining kids, about nuclear disarmament, even about Iowa's farm crisis, from "Donahue." I think it was the first place I finally figured out which country was which in the Middle East. That helped a lot at the end of the summer, when Saddam Hussein invaded Kuwait, and Steven's brother Matt shipped out with the marines.

The "Donahue" producers had sent a limousine to pick us up at the airport, and once again I gawked through the windows as we rode into the city. I could never really feel at home in such a place—the crowds, and the noise, and the speed at which everybody moved and talked were overwhelming. But it sure fascinated me.

It was almost one-thirty in the morning when we checked into our hotel, The Drake. Jeannie and I decided it might be a good idea just to go off to our rooms and go to bed, so we said good night.

About fifteen minutes after I'd gotten into my pajamas, the phone rang. It was Jeannie P., calling me from her room.

"Are you hungry?" she asked. I, of course, said yes.

"Oh, goody. Let's order up something from room service. I'll be right there," she said.

I opened my door and cautiously stuck my head out to see her running down the hall in her pajamas, quickly looking over her shoulder to make sure nobody saw. My friend the dignified lawyer, in the hall of a New York hotel, in her pajamas.

We looked over the menu, trying to make up our minds. When we decided, we called and ordered. In fact, we ordered a lot. We ordered food that looked and sounded and tasted like it was out of a movie. Shrimp cocktail; fancy marinated chicken breast salad; fresh, warm rolls; and at least a pound of butter. Lobster fettucine, wine, and huge, miraculous slabs of New York cheesecake!

Before we ate, we arranged the beautiful plates of food in the center of the king-size bed. Then we each took snapshots of the other one, posing in pajamas in the midst of the feast. If a Martian had zoomed in through the windows, he would've known in a second that these two giggling fools were the tourists from Iowa!

We had the best intentions of cleaning our plates, just as we'd been taught. But there was a point, about halfway through, where we just collapsed on the bed, clutching our stomachs and groaning. It was the first party I'd been to in a very long time.

I looked around the beautiful hotel room, and the remains of the amazing meal, and felt so far from home.

Everything had happened so fast. I barely had any time to spend time with my children, or cook a decent meal, or even brush my teeth. I would run into the house, unpack, pack, then run out again. Mom was doing the shopping, Steven was doing the cooking, and I was trying to keep in touch with them all with one long-distance telephone call after another, first checking my watch to figure out what the time difference was in whatever time zone I was in. But it wasn't enough. I hadn't pulled a kid up on my lap for days, and couldn't remember the last cup of coffee I'd had at my own kitchen table.

Jeannie and I talked for a while, and as it got later, I got sadder. And I guess I was feeling a little guilty at making a good time out of something that had begun in such seriousness.

"You know, I'll bet my old friends won't like me much anymore," I confided to Jeannie. "I get to fly all over the country, and stay in fancy hotels, and go on 'Donahue.' I mean, everybody was so great to me after the rape, and during the trial, but now . . . They'll think I'm stuck on myself, that I've changed too much, that I'm not the same person I was."

She tried to comfort me. "Nancy, you're not the same person. Nobody could expect you to be after all this. But it's not a bad kind of change. I don't think you have to worry about the people who know you the best, the people who really care about you."

I wasn't sure how I felt about that.

"Oh, let's not think about this anymore right now," she suggested. "Let's see if there's anything good on TV."

"At two-thirty in the morning?"

"Especially at two-thirty in the morning," she laughed, hitting the buttons on the remote control. She changed the channel for a minute or so, and then landed on an old "I Love Lucy" episode.

It was the one where Ricky Ricardo finally makes it big with his band, and he and Lucy are all excited about their new success, and the money, and the fame. Then they both get real blue, worrying about whether Fred and Ethel Mertz will still like them, now that so much has changed.

At the same time, Fred and Ethel are thinking that they're not good enough for their old pals, the newly successful Ricardos. Maybe Lucy and Ricky won't want to be their friends anymore, now that they're so rich and famous.

By the end of the episode, all four of them are laughing and hugging each other in the middle of the room, swearing to be friends for life, no matter what happens to them.

I couldn't believe the coincidence, and looked over at Jeannie with my jaw hanging. She was looking back at me, with a big grin on her face.

"Any questions?" she asked.

The next afternoon I was frantically getting dressed in my room, knowing that the NBC limo would be at the hotel to get us any minute and I wasn't ready yet. It's "Donahue," I kept thinking. Oh, my God. I'm going to be on "Donahue"!

I turned quickly to take a look at myself in the mirror and didn't like what I saw. The back of my dress was still wrinkled from the suitcase—I thought I'd gotten it all steamed out. Quickly, I filled the little portable steamer with water and plugged it in again. Heat up, damn it, I whispered to the thing as it sat on the counter.

Once I saw the steam was coming out, I grabbed it and aimed in the general direction of the wrinkles. Then I let out a yelp of pain. I'd made a very big mistake. I'd scalded my backside, right through the material!

Gritting my teeth and swearing like a lumberjack, I finished up as best I could. There was no time to change, no time to feel sorry for myself. I'd just have to sit on the damage. I repaired my makeup and flew out the door to join Jeannie.

The car was waiting downstairs to take us the few blocks to Rockefeller Center, where the show is taped. The spring wind was whipping the flags around the outdoor restaurant, where the skating rink is in winter. In spite of the stinging pain in my butt, I wasn't disappointed with what I saw—everything looked just the way I had always imagined it would.

I was a little more at ease about this appearance than I had been about the others. The show has a tradition of letting victims speak out. They know they will be heard, and treated with respect. Now I would become a part of that tradition.

In addition to the rape, we were also going to discuss the newspaper series, and Jane Schorer was there, too. We sat on the stage together, while Jeannie sat out in the audience. We talked first about the rape, and then about the time before and during the trial while Jane was working to put the story together.

I was grateful to see that Phil had a copy of the series in his hand, all marked up in black pen. His questions made it obvious that he'd read it well.

I was very conscious that there had to be many rape and sexual assault victims watching me. I could only hope that if they saw me as a strong survivor, as having made it through the bad times, it might in some way give them strength, too.

There was another rape survivor there, a woman named Sharon Konlos. Her story was absolutely terrifying. She had been shot in the face while driving her car, then dragged from the car and raped by the man who'd shot her. Then he abandoned her there, to die in the woods. She was almost totally blind as a result of the shooting, and her husband left her after that. She talked about how she wasn't angry anymore, how her life was good now, how she was strong, how she had forgiven her attacker.

As I listened to her, I thought to myself, maybe I shouldn't be up here. I'm still angry. I haven't forgiven anybody yet, and it's not likely that I will anytime soon.

We spoke about the importance of reporting the crime, about getting medical and psychological help, about not staying isolated. When someone from the audience asked me what I attributed my strength to, I told them about Steven, and realized that I was crying. Jane squeezed my hand, and I squeezed back.

As time had passed, and the day-to-day memories had begun to run together, I was coming to know just how much it had all depended on Steven. How much I had depended on him. And how he had never, never let me down. Sitting on that stage, with the lights in my eyes, missing him rolled over me like a big wave.

Toward the end of the program they opened up the telephone lines so viewers could call in. I remember one woman talking about her rape, about the fact that her attacker lived in her town. She felt so awful, she said, so embarrassed walking down the street. She was even thinking about apologizing to her family for bringing this shame down on them. I nearly flew out of my seat with frustration.

"Don't ever apologize for it! You don't have anything to apologize for!" I practically shouted. I wanted to go out there and find her somehow, and give her Dee Ann Wolfe's phone number. Dee Ann probably would've let her call collect.

This was the first time in the whole whirlwind of interviews and appearances that there was a live audience in front of me, and I could actually feel their response to me. They were so warm, so responsive, and, in an odd way, very protective. I felt that if we had been at home in Grinnell, I probably could've invited every single one back to my house for coffee.

From New York we flew up to Boston for an appearance on a local television program, "Good Day Boston."

When we arrived, there was a message for Jeannie to call Bill as soon as possible back at the office. I watched nervously as she walked away to make the call. Had something happened at home? The children, or Steven?

No, she told me when she came back. It was the premises liability hassle with Grand View. After all these months, they'd settled the damn thing. And they settled it, as I found out I would be allowed to say, in "a manner satisfactory to all parties."

It was difficult to keep my mind focused on what we were doing for the next few minutes. After a brief discussion of what had happened to me, and my reasons for going public, the hostess of the show said that the station would now be opening up their phone lines, and she would like all the sexual assault victims who were listening, who had never told anyone—not the police, not a doctor, not a family member—to please call in to the station.

Within about two minutes, they told me, the lines were so jammed they couldn't process the calls through the switchboard.

●

From Boston we were to fly down to Washington, D.C., to do two programs there. But after "Good Day Boston," we still had the whole afternoon left before we had to catch our plane.

"Let's play tourist," Jeannie suggested.

Her plan was, we would go out to Logan Airport, check our luggage early, pick up our tickets, and then come back into Boston for the rest of the day.

After we'd gotten out to the airport, we went to the Northwest ticket counter and asked to check the luggage and pick up the tickets.

"May I please see some proper identification?" the woman at the counter asked.

Jeannie took out her driver's license. And I took out the brand new copy of that week's *Time* magazine, the one with my picture in it. I put it down on the counter. Jeannie looked at me, totally mortified.

The woman looked at the picture, then looked back at me.

"You're her," she said. "Would you wait just a minute, please?" Then she walked away, carrying our tickets and the magazine.

In a few moments, she came back, and handed back the magazine, and our plane tickets. She had upgraded us both to first class.

We stammered out a poor attempt at a proper thank-you. Jeannie still looked mortified. I was stunned. I had given in to the old temptation to be a smart-ass and someone had really called my bluff.

So on we went through the sky, from Boston to Washington, D.C., for "CBS Nightwatch," and then on to "Crossfire" at CNN. My head was spinning, trying to keep up with where we were and what we were doing, trying to keep my answers consistent and my grammar up to Jeannie P.'s standards.

For the CNN session, I was astonished and a little nervous

to see that Wilbert Tatum, from New York's *Amsterdam News*, was there, too.

As our little "debate" progressed, it became quite heated, and so did I. Tatum went further and further with his charges that much of the underlying cause for all the tension surrounding these issues was really racism. There it is again, I thought, the wrong label on the wrong issue. It just made me so damn mad.

"There was a racist in my car the day I was raped, Mr. Tatum," I replied angrily, "but it sure wasn't me!"

CHAPTER TWENTY-SIX

AFTER MORE INTERVIEWS —The "Jane Wallace Show" on Lifetime, in New York, and the *Baltimore Sun*, along with a trip to Baltimore for that city's Rape Awareness Week at the end of April—there were a couple of things scheduled that were closer to home—and dearer to my heart. One was the "Take Back the Night" march in Des Moines.

"Take Back the Night" is a tradition that began some years ago on college campuses, where the women students and faculty would gather at nightfall to hear speakers, sing songs, and then march through the grounds of their campus, literally "taking back the night" and claiming it for everyone. The tradition has grown beyond campuses, and now there are marches taking place almost everywhere. Men often march now, too, and so do children.

My first "Take Back the Night" march was an amazing thing to be in the middle of. I was nervous at first; where are we, I wondered as we walked in the dark with flashlights and candles. Who's in charge here, anyway? But it didn't take long before I got caught up in the meaning of the march, and the sheer joy of it. To walk through the streets at night, singing and laughing and chanting, and not be afraid was something I had never experienced even before the rape, let alone after. There are fraternity brothers and bowling teams and off-duty firemen who do it all the time, and take it for granted. But there are women who know better, and do it only once a year, during a "Take Back the Night" march. They use the combined strength of their voices to bring one sad fact to a community's attention, and that is: There are certain places, certain times of day or night, where half the population is usually safe, and the other half is usually not.

We owe it to ourselves and our sons and daughters to make our communities safe for every citizen, regardless of gender. A "Take Back the Night" march can be a good way to get the attention of local politicians, the ones who control police budgets (and decide how many police ride around in patrol cars and how many walk beats); the ones who are in charge of burnt-out streetlight bulbs being replaced; the ones who see that overhanging trees and bushes are cut back so that hiding in shadows is made more difficult.

Steven and I went to the Des Moines march as ordinary participants, and to hear Geneva Overholser, who was the guest speaker that night.

After Geneva spoke, she introduced another woman. As she walked up to the microphone, it was clear that she was hugely pregnant.

"A long time ago, I was raped," the woman said. "And recently, the man who raped me came up for parole. I knew I could go to the parole hearing, and make a plea that he not be let back out on the streets. I could tell them, as I did in the trial, about what this man had done to my life. And the odds were pretty good that the parole board would pay attention to what I would say there.

"But I'm married now, with a new life, and a baby coming soon. So I thought it would be better to put it all behind me. I decided not to go to the hearing. Besides, the truth is, I was just plain scared to be in the same room with this man, to have to face him again."

She had started crying now, and I was hanging on to Steven, leaning forward to hear the rest of her story.

"And then," she said, "the weekend before the parole hearing, I read Nancy Ziegenmeyer's story in the *Des Moines Register*. And I decided that if she could do that, I could go to the parole hearing and speak my piece. So I did. And his parole was denied."

Now I was crying, too, and people were looking at me.

"Please come up to the microphone, Nancy," she said.

I slowly walked up to the microphone, trying to think of something coherent to say. I stood there for what seemed like a long time, but I was so moved by what she had said, I couldn't think of where to begin.

"My husband," I finally blurted out, "is here with me tonight, and I think he's probably pretty amazed right now. This is the very first time, in all our years together, that he's ever seen me at a loss for words!"

Little by little I had begun to get a little braver about traveling by myself and making each appearance without having a hometown face in the audience. I hated staying in hotels and motels alone, and would do almost anything to avoid it, but if I had to, I just toughed it out. But I would never take a room on the ground floor, and I needed to be close to the elevators. And the more locks on the doors, the better. I was getting very good at persuading desk clerks to change their original room plans.

In early May, I drove alone down to the National Victim Center in Fort Worth, Texas. I had been spending a lot of time on the phone with Cindy Arbelbide, the librarian at the Victim Center's astonishing resource library. When I first started putting my notebooks together, they were filled with information I was getting from Cindy. Now she had invited me to Fort Worth to meet with her and other people from the center in preparation for a conference they would be holding in Kansas City that coming summer.

The National Victim Center is, as its letterhead states, "an advocacy and resource center founded in honor of Sunny von Bulow." It was established by Mrs. von Bulow's two children,

Alexander von Bulow and Ala von Bulow Isham, and serves almost as an umbrella organization to other, more familiar advocacy groups, such as Mothers Against Drunk Driving, the National Center for Missing and Exploited Children, the National Committee for Prevention of Elder Abuse, and Parents of Murdered Children.

That's a pretty grim list, but the people in these organizations are not grim. They are strong and smart, and determined. They know as much about crime as anyone in the Justice Department, and they've learned over time where to go to seek answers—and solutions—to the problems they've faced firsthand.

As I drove to Texas that day, I kept looking at the dashboard clock. I was supposed to have a radio interview that afternoon, with CFCF Radio, a station in Montreal, Quebec. The way we'd set it up was, I would call them at a prearranged time, after I'd gotten down there and checked into my hotel. The interview would be broadcast live, and there might be a call-in question-and-answer session.

We had been getting a lot of violent spring weather in the Midwest, and the sky had looked threatening for hours, almost since I'd left Grinnell that morning. I was about thirty minutes south of Oklahoma City, in the foothills of southern Oklahoma, when the horizon went pitch black and all hell broke loose.

The thunder was roaring, and there was lightning crackling everywhere, and the GrandAm just pitched from side to side in the wind. It was one of the ugliest storms I'd ever been in in my whole life.

I'd had the windows rolled up most of the trip. Now the windshield got all steamy, and the air inside the car was clammy and stale. Suddenly I could smell my rapist all around me, in the seats, in the carpet. The highway was really hilly, and I was stuck in the center lane, unable to see well enough to pull over. The big eighteen-wheelers that rule the interstate were just slamming past me on both sides. They were Bobby's brothers, pushing me, crowding me, following me down the highway.

I was hyperventilating. It felt as if the only thing that kept me from levitating was my seat belt. I rolled the window down and took deep breaths of air as I drove.

The storm was raging, and my hair got soaked as the wind and rain blew into the car. The hills, these trucks, are all the obstacles I have to overcome, I thought. This is adversity, and I just have to get through it. I was hanging on to the steering wheel so tight I could feel the muscles bunch up in my shoulders. My God, I was scared. And, even for me, I was driving way too fast.

I heard flash-flood warnings on the radio just as I approached Dallas. I checked the clock again and saw that the storm had cost me a lot of time. I wouldn't be able to get to my hotel for the interview—I'd have to call the Canadian radio station from a pay phone someplace, and I'd have to do it in about five minutes.

I pulled into a gas station, and asked the young man who came out of the office to fill the car up. There was a pay phone just a few feet away, and I could call from there.

The sky overhead was beginning to clear as I got out of the car. My legs were wobbly, and it was hard to get my hands unclenched.

I walked to the telephone, took out a piece of paper with the telephone number on it, and made the call. The station answered and, once I identified myself, they put the host of the program on the line. I turned to lean against the pay phone, and saw that a car was pulling up to where I was standing.

It would be generous to describe the car as a little banged up. Steven worked on old cars all the time, but I had never seen anything like this. It was a wreck, and it had what I decided were bullet holes in one door, and in the hood. There were two guys sitting in the front seat. After the car had come to a stop, they just sat there. And looked at me.

"Can you hang on just one second, please?" I said to the

man on the other end of the phone. Without waiting for his answer, I dropped the phone, leaving it hanging by the metal cord, and ran over to the gas station attendant.

"Excuse me," I said shakily. "I have to make this phone call, and it's going to take a few more minutes, but those men over there . . . well, could you please just come and stand by me while I'm on the phone? Please?"

He was just a kid, not much more than twenty or twenty-one. He looked closely at me for just a second, and then said, "Sure."

We walked back over to the pay phone, where the scary guys still sat in their scary car. I picked up the dangling phone and said, "Hello?" I was relieved to find that Canada was still on the line.

As the interview progressed, they asked the usual questions and I gave my usual answers. The young gas station attendant had moved slightly, now standing squarely between me and the guys in the car. They were still sitting there, and they were still staring at me, but if I positioned myself just right, I couldn't see them.

The radio interview went on for about ten minutes, and sometime in the middle of it, the two men in the car drove off. Maybe all they'd wanted to do was use the phone, I thought.

As the interview ended and I hung up the phone, I turned and saw the expression on the young man's face. He was white as paste. I had been so scared of the guys in the car that it hadn't occurred to me that this kid would have to stand there and listen to the entire story of the rape, the aftermath, the newspaper story, and all the rest. He looked absolutely horrified at what he'd heard.

Embarrassed at what I'd put him through, I thanked him over and over, and held out a five-dollar bill for his help. But he just shook his head.

"No, ma'am," he said. "I couldn't take that from you. But I do think I'll go into the station now, and call my wife. I

haven't heard from her since I left this morning. I just need
. . . to see if she's OK."

When I finally got to my motel, I discovered they'd booked
me into a ground-floor room. No way, I told them, and firmly
insisted that they move me to a higher floor. The desk clerk
was not pleased.

"Will a room on the tenth floor be satisfactory?" he asked.

"Thank you," I answered. "It will do."

The following week I went to Ames, Iowa, with Dee Ann
Wolfe to accept an award from the Iowa Organization for
Victims Assistance. IOVA is, as the name suggests, an organization that deals with what victims of crime need after a
crime happens: psychological and medical help, financial assistance, continuing emotional support, and, most important,
advocacy—a voice to speak for them when they can't speak for
themselves.

There were opening statements and a panel discussion and,
at the end, a candlelight vigil. Each person was asked to come
forward and light a candle in memory of or in tribute to a
victim.

I remembered what Geneva Overholser had said so often:
Sunlight is the best disinfectant. And I wondered, as one by
one each little flame was lit, what this candlelight could do in
the face of the terrible statistics: a rape every six minutes, so
many women keeping the secret. It seemed so overwhelming,
like a huge physical weight pushing us all down. I don't want
to be pushed down anymore, I thought.

Dee Ann was looking over at me. You better get up there
and light a candle, her look said.

But I didn't want to light a candle for myself. I didn't want
to be a victim anymore. In fact, I knew I wasn't one. I was
trying to move ahead, into my future, whatever it would be. I
didn't want to keep looking back over my shoulder at something I couldn't change. And then it came to me, who my
candle could be for.

"This candle," I said as I lit it, "is for the children of Bobby Lee Smith, who are victims just as much as I ever was."

By the time I got back to my seat, I was crying. So was Dee Ann. She leaned over and handed me a tissue.

"As your rape crisis counselor," she whispered, "my first obligation probably should've been to tell you this: Always wear waterproof mascara."

CHAPTER TWENTY-SEVEN

N EAR THE END OF APRIL, the *Grinnell Herald-Register*, our local paper, printed a short follow-up piece on me and the blizzard of media coverage since the *Des Moines Register* series.

The reporter interviewed me for it, and I thought I did OK. Oddly, I was a little more nervous about this one than some of the "big" ones, because, after all, this was my hometown paper, and the people who read it are the same people who've known me most of my life, the same ones I run into every day.

When the paper came out, I read the piece closely and was reasonably comfortable with it.

"I don't think I embarrassed us much," I joked with Steven. "We probably won't have to move out of town just yet."

But a few days later, just after I got back from Texas, there it was: the first negative response. It was a letter to the editor, written by a local woman. The headline on the letter was "Enough Is Enough."

"Don't you think the cow has been milked dry?" the letter-writer asked. "Using the fact that you were raped to promote yourself is just plain sick."

Cow? Sick? With all the mail that had come either to the *Des Moines Register* or directly to me, there had not been—until now—one negative letter. No nasty phone calls, no obscene messages left on the answering machine. In fact, I had received letters from the ministers of every single church in Grinnell (except from the one Steven's mother attended) saying that I'd done the right thing. They had used words like "courageous" and "brave" and "strong," and they said they and their congregations were praying for me and my family.

I hadn't ever been a churchgoer, but I liked the idea of prayers being said for us. I started thinking of them accumulating someplace, like pennies saved for a rainy day. Maybe I could draw on them during those times when I was away from home, scared and lonely, and missing my family. Or maybe I could use them to cancel out all the times I lost my patience and swore at the children, when I was too tired to pack or unpack my suitcase, or too bitchy to pay attention to Bill Olson when he was trying to help me organize my life.

But now, here was the first bad letter. It was only one, I kept muttering to myself. It was only one. Yet one was enough to make me wonder if there was anybody else out there who was thinking like this, and maybe they just hadn't gotten around to writing me yet. Maybe they were in their house, sitting at a table, writing to me right now.

In mid-May I flew alone out to California to speak at the Stanford Rape Education Project. It was a two-day trip, and once again I was confronted with a ground-floor motel room.

And this time, just moving to another room wouldn't solve the problem. All the doors in the whole place were outside doors, and all the rooms were reached by outside walkways, not inside hallways. Every single room, no matter what floor it was on, was easily accessible to anybody who wanted to walk up the stairs.

I had been learning to negotiate my way around without Steven, and without Bill and Jeannie. I could do a pretty good imitation of a mature, calm person. But when it came to the question of where I would sleep, of where I would be after it got dark, I simply could not compromise. The fear of what or who was on the other side of a door was just too terrifying.

"I'm really sorry," I said to the conference organizers. "But you'll have to move me."

Ultimately, they found me a hotel with a room on a high enough floor, with big, old-fashioned bolt locks on the door. These buildings, I've noticed, aren't so easy to find in northern California.

Until the trip to Stanford, my public appearances had been limited to the news media or to victims' service professionals. This time, I would be speaking to college students. "Real people" is how I thought of them.

Going away to school, some of the experts say, is where many of our important rites of passage take place. The first absence of curfews, the first checking account, first experiences with liquor, first experiences with sex. And for many students, both male and female, it's the first place where language, intentions, and rules can get seriously blurred, and so they often find themselves making them up as they go along.

Looking out at the students' faces, it was easy to imagine Sissy in a place like this someday, bright and hopeful, walking from class to class, happily assuming that a university campus is a safe place to be. It's a dream that every parent wants for a child. Unfortunately, it's a dream that's sometimes propped up by image-conscious university administrations who either can't handle or won't admit the increased reports of sex-related crimes on college campuses.

At first I spoke to the students primarily about my own experiences—the rape, my journey through the legal system, and going public with the story. But gradually I steered things to what I really wanted to talk about: acquaintance rape, or date rape, as it's often called. (I don't like the term *date rape*, because I think it takes something serious and makes it sound trivial.)

I once heard someone explain it this way: Stranger rape is the use of sex to get power over the victim; acquaintance rape is the use of power to get sex.

According to the available studies, acquaintance rape accounts for approximately 80 percent of all rapes. Because of its very nature—the rapist is someone you know, someone you trust, quite possibly someone you care deeply for—it's the most underreported kind of attack. It's a crime that seems to carry a unique and complex set of feelings for the victim: The closer she is to her attacker, the less likely it is that she will report him.

And historically, acquaintance rape has been the one charge most likely to be dismissed as "unfounded" by police and prosecutors. "Hey, it wasn't rape," they've said, because:

"She asked him into her apartment."

"She went to the bar with him, then got in his car afterward."

"They had been dating for six months."

"She wasn't a virgin, and she was on the pill/she carried condoms in her purse."

"She went to that fraternity party willingly."

"They were lovers, then they broke up. So they already had a sexual history."

"She ordered her own drinks, and she ordered a lot of them."

"She knew her roommate was out for the night, but she invited the guy into her apartment anyway."

And so the litany goes. But nowhere in this old familiar list of "reasons why it was all right for him to do what he did" do we see "She consented to rape."

So whatever happens happens. And then the young woman goes back to her apartment or her dorm room, and knows in her heart that something is terribly wrong. Maybe she starts having nightmares, or she jumps when someone looms up behind her. She takes a lot of showers. She gets sick to her stomach when she sees the guy a few days later, because she realizes he's in her English Literature class and there's no way to avoid him.

Maybe she feels guilty about what happened, because she thinks it was probably all her fault. And she feels terrified at the idea of telling anyone, exposing herself to ridicule and blame. So she decides, by sheer force of will, that she'll forget it, or pretend it never happened. She'll take a semester off, or perhaps she'll just transfer to another school.

And then weeks or months later, when her inability to concentrate causes her to flunk out, or the eating disorder gets out of control, or the substance abuse lands her in the hospital, maybe she'll discover that her very survival depends on calling the thing what it is: rape.

"Let me put it to you as simply as I can," I said to them. "If he wants to have sex with you, and you want to have sex with him, then you must take clear and equal responsibility for that decision.

"But if he wants to have sex with you and you do *not* want to have sex with him, and you say no, and he ignores you, or pretends he doesn't hear you, or he overrules you, or he just doesn't give a damn about what you're saying at that point and goes ahead anyway: You've been raped. What has happened to you is just as serious as what happened to me. And you have a right to psychological and medical care, and a right to go to the police. And I have a responsibility to tell you, none of this will be easy."

After my talk, as the room emptied, the few young women who had lingered behind came up to speak with me. I guessed what was going on inside them by the look on each face, and I was pretty sure of what I was about to hear.

"Mrs. Ziegenmeyer," they each said quietly, "that's what happened to me. But I never knew it was rape."

CHAPTER TWENTY-EIGHT

T
HE FIRST WEEK OF JUNE, Steven and I left the three
children with my mother and drove together to Kansas City, Missouri, for the National Victim Center's "Advocacy in Action" regional conference.

It was the first time the two of us had been away alone in a
very long while. We were going to stay at a hotel at the Crown
Center, where the conference was being held, and I had been
invited to give the keynote speech at the luncheon on Saturday.

Maybe it wouldn't be everybody's idea of a fantasy honey-
moon trip, but it was for us. It was also the anniversary of our
wedding—after what we had gone through, that date was
something worth commemorating.

Maybe we would go out for all our meals, and then sit in the
restaurant and talk for a long time after dessert if we felt like it.
Let someone else worry about the cooking, let someone else
make the bed. Maybe we could even go shopping. And maybe
I could get him to hold hands with me in public, even though
we weren't in a courtroom.

The trip to Kansas City took about four hours. On the way
we stopped at a bookstore in Des Moines where I picked up
some books that had been recommended to me, on sexual
assault and marital rape. They weren't light reading for a vacation weekend, they were part of what I'd be expected to

discuss at the conference, and part of the ever-growing collection of books we were making room for back home.

I drove for a while, with the windows down and the music playing. It was the most beautiful day. Unlike last year, the spring and early summer had been very rainy, and the fields all the way from Iowa to Missouri were incredibly green.

When Steven took the wheel, I read aloud from the books we'd bought. At the conference, we'd be spending time with people whose business it was to work with all this information, and Steven had become as determined as I was to learn as much as possible about the facts, figures, and horror stories.

There would be some old friends there: Dee Ann Wolfe, and Marti Anderson, from the Des Moines Crime Victim Assistance Program, and Cindy Arbelbide, the center's librarian who had been my hostess in Fort Worth. I had first met each of them when I was at my lowest point. Now I would be with them not as a victim but as a survivor, and a fellow victims' advocate.

The other people attending this conference were not just victim service professionals and volunteers, but also doctors, nurses, police, psychologists, and educators. And many of them were survivors of violent crime, with information that I needed to hear as to what had gone wrong in our society, and what part I could play to begin to make it right.

One thing had become clear to me over the past year: The more I thought I knew about rape and all its complications, side effects, and aftermath, the more I still had to learn. There were as many stories as there were victims.

The first workshop I attended at the conference was on sexual assault. The notes I took that day have exclamation points, stars, and asterisks all over them—I couldn't write fast enough to keep up with all the issues that were being raised by the speakers. They ranged from the smallest detail of medical care to the biggest wrestling matches in public policy. For instance:

- sweatsuits for victims: which hospitals supply them, what to do if your local hospital doesn't, and where the funding comes from—or more likely these days, where it doesn't come from.

- a private bathroom and shower for rape victims, to clean up after rape exams: which hospitals supply them, how to organize to get your hospital to provide one.

- the lack of mental health professionals who are specialists in sexual assault, which often results in therapy that's not specific to the problems of the rape victim.

- ego problems among the professionals: competition among the police, the medical/therapeutic community, and the criminal justice system. Literally, "Who's in charge here?" and how we can get them all to cooperate and collaborate.

- the rapid increase in juvenile sexual assaults: two main issues. One, that the aftermath treatment for juveniles must be significantly different than for adults, and once again that leads to the problems of therapy that is not victim-specific. Second, victims as perpetrators: Just as we've seen with physical child abuse, a sexually abused young person is statistically likely to grow up and become a victimizer. This is the one area where prevention might really be possible.

- police department attitudes: Do your local and state police receive any specialized training in the academies or on the job about dealing with sexual assault victims? If so, how much, and is it enough? If not, how to go about changing the status quo.

- the pros and cons of going through the criminal justice system versus civil litigation—that is, suing the attacker for depriving you of your civil rights.

- organizing your community around prevention: things like getting streetlights repaired as soon as they go out, foliage trimmed so attackers can't hide, being involved in the educational process with high school students, knowing the crime statistics in your town, and lobbying for police to walk a beat or be on visible patrol in their cars.

•

After a few hours of soaking up this kind of information, I felt like a sponge at full capacity. There was so much to do, and so much to learn from people who had confronted each one of these problems in their own communities, and had somehow found the will and the tools to solve them.

Many of them were caring professionals, but many more had themselves been victims. They didn't talk in stiff, academic language, or even try to maintain objectivity. They spoke with anger and passion about what they knew.

It made me consider the word *witness* in a whole new light, for it was clear these people were witnesses: They were the ones who knew the truth and had the courage to tell it. Survivors of rape and incest, peace officers who could solve crimes but were often helpless to prevent them: To me, they looked like an army in a war that seemed unwinnable. Yet they kept on fighting.

Later that afternoon I tried to absorb yet another mass of information, this time about DNA and sexually transmitted diseases that result from sexual attacks.

I was certainly familiar with all the complications associated with using DNA evidence in a trial, but one problem raised was something I'd overlooked: The laboratory testing procedures are expensive, and reduced budgets mean that prosecutors have to pick and choose which cases to spend this money on.

This was, after all, the early summer of 1990—no one was using the term *recession* yet, and the effects of mangled federal and state budgets were only beginning to surface. But it was easy to imagine a criminal case where introducing DNA evidence could make a big difference in the verdict, and yet the prosecution would be prevented from doing so because there was no money available.

In the area of sexually transmitted disease, the biggest worry, of course, was AIDS—technically HIV. More and more, crisis counselors reported, the first question victims were asking them is "Will I get AIDS?" And the truthful answer each time must be, "We don't know."

The length of time between exposure to HIV and the development of the antibodies in the blood that would show up in testing is a minimum of six weeks to three months. But the infection itself can't be ruled out for years—as long as nine years after an attack, some experts are now saying.

Although the likelihood of contacting HIV after only one exposure is low (the professionals call exposure "dose-related"), that's small comfort to a victim. The testing must be done immediately, and repeated several times afterward, over a long period—for the rest of your life, some women say.

I've continued to have the test regularly myself, every six months since my rape. It caused some real embarrassment when we switched family doctors and I had to explain why I wanted it.

The test can range from being moderately costly to very expensive, and the question always is: Who pays? Victim reparation or compensation funds will usually pay for one test, but every six months for eight or ten years? And what if a victim didn't report the crime? What if her insurance company draws the line, or what if she's too traumatized even to ask her local doctor for the test?

Some victims are now asking to take the drug AZT (in spite of the absence of symptoms or positive test results) as a precaution, in much the same way they would ask for the morning-after birth control treatment. If a woman opts to take AZT as a precautionary measure (after considering the fact that it's a highly toxic drug and might affect her ability to have children), how will she pay for it?

And, of course, the questions don't get less complicated once the police find and arrest the attacker, because of the constitutional guarantee of his right to privacy versus mandatory testing. Laws differ from state to state, but for the most part, you can't force a suspect to take an HIV test.

Once there's a conviction, many prisons mandate the test

before they admit someone into the prison population, but that won't do a victim any good: She can't find out whether he tested positive or negative because that's considered confidential information.

I thought of the story I'd heard about one victim of rape, whose attacker later died in prison of an AIDS-related illness. She couldn't even find out if he'd tested positive for the disease when he was initially convicted, or if he'd contacted the disease after he got to prison. After all, one lawyer said, no matter how or when a rapist contacted the disease, knowing was really only a "peace of mind" issue for a victim. He said "only peace of mind" in the same tone he would've said "only a hangnail."

Other issues involved how probable it is that a victim might develop a substance-abuse problem in the aftermath of an attack. Liquor, sleeping pills, tranquilizers, even recreational drugs—a victim may be very likely to use anything that might "medicate" the pain and the terror. And suicide! Studies show that one out of five sexual assault victims try to kill themselves.

My mood roller-coastered all day long. That could've been me, I would think, hearing one horror story after another. Yet here I was, intact, safe, eager to become part of the solution. How on earth had I been so lucky?

During my talk at the luncheon, it was good to look out at the audience sitting at the tables and see Steven there. I was becoming more comfortable telling my story, and I especially trusted these people. They were, in the truest sense, my support group, and it was only right that my husband be among them.

When I mentioned his name, and the role that he played in my recovery, some turned and looked at him. For his part, he looked back at me, and then down at his dessert. He has always maintained that what he had done and how he had behaved was "no big deal." There were men and women in that room who knew better.

That night, there was an incredible thunderstorm, with lightning that lit up our room and filled the sky for as far as we could see. Steven held me as we stood at the window and watched as wave after wave rolled through Kansas City, and we listened to the thunder echo off the buildings. I was a long way from where it all started, but the information in my beat-up old notebooks told me that there was still a long, long way to go.

CHAPTER TWENTY-NINE

O NCE AGAIN, I was out on the road by myself, driving north to Lake Okoboji, Iowa. As usual, I had a full supply of chocolate, the country station on the radio cranked at full volume, and all four doors locked.

I was going to meet Nan Horvat at the Iowa State Prosecutors Spring Conference, where we were going to deliver a joint presentation about "our" rape case. Nan would be speaking specifically about the use of DNA evidence in prosecuting these cases.

Okoboji's a beautiful resort on the Iowa/Minnesota state line, and I had been looking forward to the trip since the invitation had first arrived. This would be the first time since the trial that Nan and I would be doing something almost as colleagues, and I had my good suit, safe in its dry-cleaner bag, hanging in the back of the car. All the prosecuting attorneys from Iowa would be there for their week-long conference, and it was important that they take me seriously.

When I got to the motel where the conference had booked me, I was once again taken aback by the location of the room. Ground floor, outside corner, too many windows, every one of them open. But it had a wonderful view of the lake, with a dock and a beach just steps away. I took a deep breath and decided to stay in the room.

It took just about twenty minutes to change out of my

shorts and into my giving-a-speech-to-important-lawyers out-
fit, and then I raced off to where the first meeting of the
conference would be held.

Nan was already there, and we compared notes for a few
minutes as the room began to fill up. I quickly saw I'd made
a major mistake wearing a suit and heels. Everyone was in
shorts, T-shirts, baseball caps, fishing hats, sneakers, sandals.
The room was warm, and got warmer as more and more
people came in and sat down.

It was nearly six, and I realized with a sinking heart that Nan
and I were going to be all that stood between these vacationing
lawyers and their cocktail hour and dinner. I didn't feel any
better when I found out that, in addition to our presentation,
there would also be remarks and a question-and-answer period
for the two candidates for state's attorney general. Right away,
it felt all wrong.

Although I was introduced very graciously, I fervently began
to wish I was someplace else. The faces in the auditorium
looked impassively back at me as I talked about my dismay at
finding out it was not "my" case but that, instead, I was only
a witness for the state of Iowa. So what else is new, their
lawyerly expressions seemed to say.

I had given enough speeches and presentations over the past
few months to begin to read the reactions of audiences. But
here, as I spoke about the delays, and the attitude of the FBI,
and the continuances, nothing came back to me from those
who were listening.

I talked about my constant feeling that the rights afforded to
the defendant did not extend to me, the victim, and how
vulnerable and frustrated this had made me feel. And how,
although I really respected Nan's expertise and knew she'd
done a good job for me, I had wished there had been some
kind of victims' advocate there just for me, to explain the
justice system's inner workings to me, and maybe explain me
to the justice system.

There seemed to be no air left in the room at all. I was

sweating, and my notes were shaking in my hand. It felt exactly like high school, standing there delivering a report that I'd worked all night on but that nobody in the class really wanted to hear.

When I had completed my remarks, there was scattered applause, and then the noise of people shifting and fidgeting in metal folding chairs. The smell of coffee drifted in from the lobby, and I saw a couple of people look longingly toward the door.

Nan then went on and gave her talk about DNA, both about the way it had figured in her prosecution of this case and the way it was being used in cases all over the country. As I sat next to her at the table and looked out over the room, it seemed that more people were paying attention to her than had paid attention to me.

"This science is going to become an invaluable tool. And as prosecutors, you will have to understand it," she told them firmly. "And once you understand it, you're going to have to explain it to the jury, so they can understand it. And you're going to have to be prepared for the defense to jump all over you." She even had a couple of good one-liners in there that got laughs, something that I had decided would be inappropriate for me to do.

Soon enough—but not soon enough for me—it was over, and the two candidates for attorney general, both of whom I'd already met, delivered their campaign remarks. When their question-and-answer period began, I signaled "See you later" to Nan, slipped out the door as discreetly as I could, and headed for my car.

Once out on the sidewalk, I took a deep breath. That was truly the presentation from hell, I thought to myself. And then I heard someone running up behind me, calling my name. I turned, and found myself facing a young woman, out of breath and flushed from the heat.

"Uh, Nancy. I mean, Mrs. Ziegenmeyer," she said. "I just wanted to tell you, I think what you did was so brave. The newspaper thing, I mean. I'm a lawyer, and I hope, sometime, that more witnesses will be like you. It's so important to be strong and get involved like that." She had tears in her eyes as she spoke. "And maybe, this will all change things somehow," and she gestured toward the auditorium I'd just left.

"Thank you" was all I could manage.

When I got back to the motel, I quickly changed out of my suit and went off to find a restaurant. Food would make me feel better, I thought, and maybe a drink. I would calmly watch the sunset over the lake, and smoke a cigarette or two, and find a way to put it all in some kind of perspective.

After I'd eaten, I walked back toward my room. It was nearly dark, and the mayflies had come up over the lake, little green biting things that swarmed around my head. I heard laughter coming from the rooms on either side of mine, and more laughter coming up from the dock. When I stepped inside, I just knew I couldn't stay there.

I went to the clerk and said there was an emergency at home, and I had to check out early. He looked right through me.

The drive back to Grinnell took nearly five hours. I gassed up the car, picked up a couple of Cokes and some more chocolate, and put the Meat Loaf *Bat Out of Hell* tape into the cassette player.

I got home around three and had to bang on the front door to wake Steven and get him to come down and let me in. I was so tired I was nearly cross-eyed, but I didn't care. Being home was worth it. Being home was worth anything.

That spring, Senator Joseph Biden of Delaware had proposed new legislation to "reduce the growing problem of violent crime against women." Senator Biden, who chairs the Senate Judiciary Committee, called this legislation "The Violence Against Women Act of 1990."

I was invited to Washington in late June to testify before the Senate Judiciary Committee.

Of all the invitations I had received, of all the appearances I had made, this one was the most important. The idea of going before members of our government and actually speaking to them both terrified and inspired me. Terror, because these were the Big Boys: the people in charge of making the laws. Inspiration, because it seemed they were going to make this particular law based on what they heard from women who had been victims of crime.

All along, what I had wanted most was for someone to listen. But I couldn't have asked for an audience more powerful than this one. Once again, I was reevaluating what it meant to be a witness.

I wanted Jeannie P. to come with me, but Bill decided that he would go and sit at the table with me. While I respected his judgment in most things, I regretted his decision a little: It was clear there would be no pajama-party food-feast to calm my nerves on this trip.

I had been told that I would have about five minutes to deliver any remarks for the record, and then Senator Biden and the other members of the committee would ask me questions. Steven and I worked for days on what I would say, knowing that this speech would be read into the Congressional Record, and might possibly be part of the decision-making on the wording of the bill. Maybe something that I could tell them would be part of convincing other legislators to actually support this bill, to vote it into law.

Bill and I got to the Des Moines airport early on the morning of June 19. It was while we were waiting for our connection to Chicago that we suddenly heard his name being called out over the loudspeaker.

He went off to find out what the problem was, and then came back to inform me that NBC news was calling: They knew I was on my way to testify and wanted me to be on the "Today" show the next morning.

I couldn't believe it. There was just something crazy, even frightening, about the fact that I could be standing in an airport like any other passenger and, just like that, somebody could track me down.

Bill speculated that maybe NBC had spoken to someone from Senator Biden's office, or called Bill's law office or my house, and Steven or someone else had probably explained where we were and how to get hold of us.

What he said made perfectly good sense. But I still had a queasy stomach. Part of it was being found like that at the airport—it was too weird. Part of it, I knew, was the very idea that tomorrow morning, at this same time, I'd be sitting in front of a bunch of senators trying to talk them into passing national legislation.

When we arrived at our hotel, the Washington National on Capitol Hill, I was glad to see that my room was sufficiently above the first floor, with a nice, big, shiny hunk of metal on the door for a lock.

The next morning, as Bill and I walked into the room where the hearings would be held, we were both almost blinded by the television lights. Bill had his hand firmly under my arm, and he steered me to my seat. Blinking, I looked around, trying to get my bearings.

Senator Biden opened the hearings with a quote from President Franklin D. Roosevelt that listed one of the "Four Essential Human Freedoms"—the Freedom from Fear.

"Does a woman in this country," Senator Biden asked, "enjoy that essential freedom? The freedom to walk down a street and not fear that someone will follow her, or rob her, or perhaps even rape her; the freedom to walk in grocery store parking lots; to jog in public parks; to ride in city buses? I suspect that many women in this country today would say that they do not."

And he went on. "During the last ten years, the rape rate has risen four times faster than the national crime rate. Assaults against young women have reached an all-time high: rising 50 percent over the last decade and a half, while the rate for assaults against young men has actually declined."

His proposed legislation had three basic goals: to make streets safer for women; to make homes safer for women; and to protect women's civil rights.

To support the need for the legislation, Senator Biden introduced statistics, some of which were familiar to me, some of which were new. Among them: A woman is ten times more likely to be raped than to die in a car crash; one-third of all domestic violence cases, if reported, would be charged as felony rape or felonious assault; the rape rate in the United States is thirteen times higher than England's, four times higher than Germany's, twenty times higher than Japan's.

The proposed legislation addressed increased penalties and victim restitution; increased funding of law-enforcement grants to train additional police, prosecutors, and victim advocates; capital improvement grants for lighting and camera surveillance at public waiting places; and establishing a National Commission on Violent Crime Against Women, modeled on the AIDS commission, to help focus attention on these crimes. In addition, it would: create federal penalties to prosecute abusers who cross state lines to escape prosecution; double the funding for battered women's shelters; and define gender-motivated crimes as "bias" crimes, which would then create a civil rights remedy based on existing civil rights laws.

I was understandably nervous as I gave my prepared remarks. It was hard not to be distracted by what I'd just heard: a dream list of remedies that would address almost everything that had been discussed at the National Victim Center conference. How could anyone argue against this, I wondered? Could my statement actually contribute to this legislation becoming a reality? And where on earth would the money for it come from?

Senator Charles Grassley, one of Iowa's senators, spoke for a few minutes to the committee, telling them of his pride in me, a fellow Iowan. And then, after a few remarks from Senator Howard Metzenbaum of Ohio, I began to deliver my prepared remarks.

Essentially, I told them the story of what had happened to

me and, afterward, what had happened to our lives as a family. I spoke of my frustration with the legal system, my appreciation for the support and advocacy of the crisis center, and my deep gratitude for the role Steven had played in encouraging me to speak out. "My assailant tried to take away the control I had over my own life," I told them. "I am determined he will not succeed."

There was another crime survivor testifying that morning. Her name was Marla Hansen, and she was from New York.

Marla Hansen was an aspiring model and actress whose case got into the national news in a particularly awful way. She had been pressured by her landlord, who wanted to take her out. When she turned him down, and then decided it was in her best interest to move out of the apartment she was renting from him, he hired three thugs to grab her in the street and cut up her face with razor blades.

All the men involved in this terrifying crime were eventually convicted, but not before Marla had to go through a trial in which the defense attorney, Alton Maddox, tried to portray her to the jury as completely responsible for her own wounds. She was racist (her attackers were black), he said, and she was a sexual tease. It was her provocative behavior, plus the clothes she wore, that brought the attack down upon her.

The judge had allowed the defense lawyer to make these accusations and, as Marla said to the members of the committee in her testimony, "The psychological violence I endured throughout the trial was far more traumatizing to me than the attack on the street."

Although my experience was vastly different from hers, much of what she said that morning was achingly familiar.

I looked at the men seated at the table in front of me: Senator Biden, Senator Grassley, Senator Metzenbaum, Senator Strom Thurmond from South Carolina, and Senator Arlen Specter from Pennsylvania.

I only hoped, as I watched and listened carefully to them responding first to me and then to Marla, that in us they saw their wives, their sisters, their daughters. As they asked each of us questions about our encounters with the judicial system, I hoped that it would not take the victimization of someone they loved to give them the will to pass this legislation.

Maybe my being here will be my gift to my daughter, I thought. Maybe Sissy will grow up in a world where these crime statistics will shrink instead of grow, gradually becoming part of a history that she will not ever, ever need to experience.

CHAPTER THIRTY

IN DES MOINES, a battle had started that I didn't ever think I'd be fighting. Geneva Overholser had discovered that the city police department had a policy of routinely withholding rape victims' names from the *Register's* police reporter.

Even though she claimed that the paper would never publish the names without asking the victim's permission, she threatened to sue the police, under the Freedom of Information Act, if they continued to follow this policy. She wanted those names treated like any other names in a police department crime report: available to the press. And available, I guessed, to anyone else who marched into the police department and asked for them.

What if an attacker had threatened the victim, and then discovered, by reading the *Des Moines Register* the next day, that she'd gone to the police? Or what if, in the case of a stranger rape, he attacked her in a parking lot, as my attacker did, and then found out her name and home address in the paper the next day? How convenient, especially if he wanted to go back and finish her off.

This was a First Amendment issue, everyone said. In a democracy, the police shouldn't be the ones to decide what gets reported and what doesn't, everyone said. But what about the victim, I asked. Shouldn't the victim be a major part of that decision?

All the victims' support groups in Iowa rallied around, protesting what seemed to be an insensitive move on Geneva's part. More than one rape victim said, "If I had thought for one moment that a reporter or anyone else could have found out who I was and what happened to me, or that someone could contact me for a story and my name would be in print, I would never have reported my rape to the police." Me neither.

We started lobbying the Iowa legislature to formulate a confidentiality bill. It would keep the identity of rape and sexual assault victims confidential, for a specific period of time—at least until there was an arrest and an indictment.

I believed that what I had done in going to the *Register* and telling my story had been the right decision—for me. To speak out, to put a voice and a face to a crime that nobody wanted to acknowledge—that was important. But the idea that a reporter could've gone ahead and written something about me (Geneva's best intentions notwithstanding) without my knowing, without my permission, without my being part of it, just scared the hell out of me. Why not just make the victim parade naked through the streets?

I wrote to Geneva. I called the attorney general's office. I called the governor's office, and then I called the guy who was running against him. I wrote letters to everyone I could think of, joined the lobbying effort, talked to reporters.

Yes, I said, it is important for victims to come forward, if they decide they can do that. But if they do, they should be allowed to do so in their own time, under their own steam, when they've had time to heal, as I had. They shouldn't be forced into the sunlight until they're ready.

Why was that so complicated? Why did a woman's need to heal in peace and private have to go head to head with the Constitution?

The summer was racing by us in a blur of interviews, trips, speeches, and frantic logistics problems to solve.

I woke up almost every morning long before the alarm went

off, jump-starting myself into the day, sure that I'd already fallen behind. I had to make a costume for Sissy's dance recital and get after the boys about piano practice. I had to get my flowers planted in the garden, and we needed to carve out a weekend somewhere so that Steven and I could finish painting the outside of the house.

It was a project that had been abruptly interrupted when I was raped, and the house had been half-yellow, half-beige for more than a year. Plus, we'd gutted the living and dining rooms, there was dry wall and plaster dust everywhere, and we still hadn't managed a vacation.

And always, there was the mail to answer, and messages from Bill Olson on the answering machine.

It got harder and harder to make time for my family. I would stay awake at night, staring at the ceiling, thinking of everything I'd said and done that day that had fallen short of what the kids needed from me. It felt as if I'd been pushing them to the bottom of my list for months. Steven and I could hold each other, we could talk late into the night, we could communicate with each other in the familiar code that promised "I'll catch up with you later." But how could I reconnect with my children?

We decided that I would take each of them along with me on the next three trips I had to make out of town. Benjamin would be the first—we would go to Denver, Colorado, for the annual meeting of the National Coalition Against Sexual Assault.

It was a relief to leave town and head for the mountains, and it felt good to have Ben along. During the day, I attended the workshops. But in the afternoons, the two of us would jump into the rental car and go exploring.

We went to Rocky Mountain National Park, and to the Denver Zoo, and to the Science Museum. We ate junk food, and watched a little TV, and just hung out. Every once in a while, I'd grab Ben and just hug him, which he tolerated with all the dignity a seven-year-old boy can muster.

At the end of the conference, we attended the National "Take Back the Night" march together. There he stood, my middle baby, right next to me at the front of the line. He wore an iridescent green T-shirt that said "What part of no don't you understand?"

In July, the *Des Moines Register* published what I came to think of as the "backlash" story.

I had been riding around in limousines, ordering lobster from room service in fancy hotels, it said. People in Grinnell didn't like me, it said. I'm taking advantage of the situation to feed my ego and my pocketbook, it said. And the truth about Steven and me was that we weren't really a normal married couple. In fact, our life was pretty messy.

What the hell were they talking about, I wondered. What was it, exactly, that made us "not normal," aside from the fact that I'd been raped? We were more normal than a lot of other couples I knew.

The *Des Moines Register* had known all along about the troubles between us, about the fact that we'd reconciled about five minutes before Bobby Lee Smith had forced his way into my car that morning. They didn't seem to think it was such a big deal when they ran the series—why was it important now? Should we have squeezed some big, fancy remarriage ceremony into our schedule over the past couple of years? Maybe between court continuances, or between the verdict and the sentencing?

"Hundreds of women are raped, and they all have to get up the next morning and get on with their lives, and take care of their kids and families. They don't go on the Donahue show or do a book and make a fortune," was the comment from one local woman—the same one, I noticed, who'd written the "enough is enough" letter a couple of months before.

But I do take care of my kids and my family, I thought. I make peanut butter sandwiches, and I occasionally vacuum (although house renovations were making it tougher and tougher). I even scrub the toilet, although I avoid it as long as I can. I make some of Sissy's clothes and cut the boys' hair. The last time I checked, nobody had hired any maids or cooks to work in my house (I'm sure I would've noticed them).

"This is not a story about rape," one man was quoted as saying to the paper. "This is a story about market economics, about a woman who saw a way to make a buck, and is taking advantage of it."

I pitched a full-steam-ahead tantrum for the next twenty minutes, without stopping once to take a breath.

Saw a way to make a buck? What does this guy think I did, anyway, drive into the parking lot at Grand View College with a sign around my neck that said, "Please rape me, my husband and I are having a little trouble making ends meet"?

Sure, in the beginning I had wanted someone to pay for what had happened to me. I thought, at the time, that it was a fairly typical human response.

Marla Hansen, for instance, filed a civil suit against her attackers, and won a *Guinness Book of World Records* figure of $78 million. Of course, she has about as much chance as a snowball in hell of ever seeing one cent, and she acknowledged that to the Senate Judiciary Committee. But she felt vindicated when she won the suit, and if there was ever a chance of her getting any compensation from the people who had hurt her, could anyone honestly begrudge her that?

And yes, Bill Olson had won the premises liability settlement from Grand View College. If Steven and I were careful, that money would send our kids to college (if that's where they wanted to go), although they'd still have to have summer jobs. Maybe it would get Steven his own garage some day. And I confess, I had plans to buy my mother a new sofa for Christmas.

But in the meantime, Steven was still only taking two weeks off a year, and I was still making Chef Boy-ar-Dee pizza for the kids.

Some of this, I knew, was about "the fame thing." I was as

perplexed about "the fame thing" as anybody, because I couldn't decide if I liked it or hated it. Steven thought it was all a huge invasion of his privacy, but me, I changed my mind just about every day.

I certainly liked having strong opinions on an issue that I thought I knew something about, and having people pay attention to me. It was hard work at first, and often frightening to me. But I liked the respect that came with it, and the self-esteem, and the way it was making what had happened to me begin to count for something positive.

But I sure didn't like being tracked down in airports. And I really didn't like it the day I was scolding the kids in Toys-R-Us in Des Moines. I looked up to see two or three people watching as I spit out every word. I just knew what they were thinking: "There's that rape victim from the 'Donahue' show, being mean to her children!"

But most of all, I would have liked not being raped in the first place.

Would I have made a more acceptable victim if I'd stayed down? If I hadn't spoken out? If I'd become a martyr rather than a survivor?

Stop this, I commanded myself. This is like all the what-ifs after the rape. What if I'd locked the car door, what if I'd fought harder, and on and on . . .

No, it's too late and too silly to waste energy on worrying about what other people think. We'd spent too many sleepless nights, with Steven walking me to the bathroom in the dark, to be stampeded by anyone who believes the best victim is either a dead one or a mute one. If I needed reminding, all I had to do was reread the letters. They were the best testimony to what I had done, and the only affirmation I needed.

In mid-August I flew to Los Angeles with Sissy to be honored as one of *Esquire* magazine's "Women We Love." The party was black tie, we were to stay at the Beverly Hills Hotel, and even the baby daughter princess was going to wear a long dress. A pink one, with pink lace tights.

"You spoil that child rotten," Steven always says. He's right, I do.

This little girl was born batting her eyelashes, but she's more like a baby pit bull than a delicate flower. If her brothers climb a tree, she follows them up. If they dig a ditch, she climbs into it with them. If they're throwing a football, she's running around trying to catch it. When either of them are in danger, she's capable of turning on kids twice her size in their defense. And she can be ruthless when crossed.

One night last summer, Steven and I saw Nick and Ben shoo Sissy away from where they were sitting in the front yard, playing with their little cars and trucks. She watched and waited until the boys, bored with what they were doing, wandered off. Then she went over, calmly dug a big hole, put their toys down into it, and filled the hole with dirt. Her father and I just looked at each other. Steven's mouth was twitching.

Sissy and I giggled a lot during our trip to Los Angeles. Getting her dressed up for the party gave me a preview of what future prom nights with Miss-Princess-of-the-World were going to be like. During the evening, I was surprised to hear that *Esquire* has donated a significant amount of money to the National Coalition Against Domestic Violence. The funds would go, it was hoped, toward maintaining shelters for battered women.

We were between courses, with waiters clearing the appetizers and bringing dinner, when Sissy opened her mouth like a sleepy cat, and let out a huge yawn. She then cleared a small place on the tablecloth, folded her arms on the table, put her head down, and went soundly to sleep, her bright curly hair narrowly missing her salad plate.

On August 18, the first verdict in the Central Park jogger case: all three defendants guilty of rape, assault, robbery, and riot. There! I whispered all the way across the country to her. There!

•

On August 22, I made the last trip of the summer, to New York City with Nicholas, to appear on the "Sally Jessy Raphael Show."

A few nights before we left, I had a weird nightmare. It seemed, in this dream, that Iowa had the death penalty, and Bobby Lee Smith had been sentenced to death. And the law said that Steven and I had to go witness his electrocution.

For some reason, the mechanics of the electric chair wouldn't work. When they took Smith back to his cell, it was already occupied by someone else, so he had to come home with me and Steven, to stay with us until the machine was fixed, and his execution could be rescheduled.

Our house, in the dream, had lots of stairways, between the floors, between the rooms. Somehow, we lost track of Bobby Lee Smith. I knew he was someplace in our house, but I couldn't find him. Steven and I ran up and down the stairs, calling out his name. I know dreams only last a minute or two in real time, but this one seemed to go on all night. I woke up in a cold sweat, in tears.

When we got to New York City, Nick's first request was to go to the Empire State Building. Our ears popped as the elevator climbed. From the top, it seemed as if we could look out and see the whole world. Other people came and went, but we stayed up there, together, with the wind blowing and the sun shining, for a long time.

Our next stop was to what a friend of mine calls "the museum." F.A.O. Schwarz, the toy store that can make a kid lose his grip in three minutes flat.

Nick's eyes grew bigger and bigger as we went through the door and walked onto the ground floor.

"One thing for you, one thing for Ben, one thing for Sissy. Small things, please," I decreed.

Nick is the child most like his dad. He took a good, long, slow look around the whole store before he made up his mind on what to take back home. He'd stop, and look, and consider, then walk some more. Then he decided: hand-held video games for him and Benjamin, and beautiful little ballet slippers for Sissy.

I was surprised, when I got to Sally Jessy Raphael's studio, to see that I'd share the stage with my least favorite debate partner, Bill Tatum, publisher of the *Amsterdam News*. I think if I had known he'd be there, I would not have appeared. From that moment on, I felt like I'd been sandbagged.

The subject for discussion was, of course, the press's treatment of rape victims. Another member of the panel was Amy Pagnozzi of the *New York Post*. Over the months, she'd written quite a bit about sexual assault and confidentiality. I even had some of her articles in my clippings file. Right away, it was clear that she was a match for Tatum. They got into it before the first commercial break!

On the night the attack on the Central Park jogger was first reported, two local New York television stations had announced her name on the air, for which they almost immediately apologized. But Tatum, on deadline and having confirmed her name with the police, decided to go ahead and print it. He claimed he only printed it twice—one each in two separate articles. Sally Jessy Raphael said that in one article alone, she counted the name used eleven times.

Also on the panel that day was Ellen Levin, mother of the young woman killed in Central Park in what came to be called the Preppy Murder Case. As with Marla Hansen, this was another situation where the victim, rather than the defendant, seemed to be on trial.

Levin has become a victims' advocate, and the constant pain she feels not just at her daughter's death but at the way she was attacked after her death is written deeply into her face.

The discussion, interrupted only now and then by questions from the audience, grew very intense. For the most part, I sat quietly and watched the New Yorkers go at it.

Tatum was calm, almost eerily so, and very self-righteous

when he talked about the Central Park jogger case, claiming at one point that he, for one, wasn't even convinced that there was a rape. When Pagnozzi challenged him on some of his facts, he responded by sweetly addressing her as "dear." I could feel my jaw tighten up.

Near the end of the program, I listened with pain as Robert Gottlieb, a defense attorney, talked about how he believed that any tactic is acceptable in a defense, even if it meant dragging a rape victim's bedsheets into the courtroom.

I finally lost my cool when Bill Tatum complained about the death threats he and his family had received since his paper had printed the jogger's name.

"You got death threats because of a decision you willingly made," I practically shouted at him. "But my family and I got death threats not because of any decision we made, not because of anything we had control over, but because of something that was forced on us!"

And then, regaining a little composure, I said, "The question of naming rape victims in the press isn't the important thing, anyway. We need not ask who the victim is—the victim is all of us!"

CHAPTER THIRTY-ONE

STEVEN'S YOUNGER BROTHER MATTHEW, a U.S. Marine, was shipped to the Persian Gulf in late summer. In mid-September, after getting the kids settled back in school, I went to Norfolk, Virginia, to spend some time with Heather, Matt's wife, who was expecting their second baby and trying to cope with Joshua, their first.

Before I left, after a long talk with Steven, I took my wedding rings to the jeweler in Grinnell who had originally made them for us.

He removed the stones from them, and he removed the little sapphires from the earrings and necklace I'd been wearing the day of the rape. He fashioned them all together in a new ring, which then went right back on my third finger, left hand. We put the old settings safely away, for Sissy.

Once in Norfolk, I was quickly caught up in someone else's household. I had forgotten—too quickly, it seemed—what it was like to be with little ones like Josh, so energetic and busy, so full of curiosity, yet quite happy to sit on a lap for a minute or two and let themselves be cuddled.

My own children, especially the boys, would rather eat dirt than be cuddled these days, although Sissy still voluntarily climbed up on Steven once in a while. Playing Annie Nanny to Josh was a great comfort, and being there for Heather while

Matt was so far away, going to the middle of God knows what, made me feel useful.

But there was often time to spare, and when it came, I would go for long walks on the beach alone. It was quiet there, far away from the mail, and the telephone, and I could think, long, loopy thoughts that had no particular beginning or end, but seemed to pull together somehow all the events of the past couple of years.

One of the letters I received after the *Register* series was from a man. He wrote:

"I am grateful that you are alive, sharing your experience for the benefit of others. When I think of you and what you are accomplishing, I am reminded of an ocean shell called 'angels' wings.' This shell is fragile enough to be crushed by an ordinary human hand, yet, because it goes with the ocean's flow, it does not crumble. It exists well below the surface of the water under tremendous pressures. It is constantly being tossed around by the currents and gale force winds and is endlessly moved along the ocean floor across rough sand. Yet, with all this adversity, it gains only a smoother and more beautiful finish."

I have referred to the words in this letter many times since I received it, and I thought about it again as I walked along the beach. While the words were written to me, they are just as much a loving tribute to all the survivors who have not been crushed by that "ordinary" human hand.

I almost allowed that hand to crush me. What gave me the strength to go from victim to survivor, and how can we pass that strength on to all the victims of this crime?

I know I have been blesssed with my husband, who is to me a hero. He could have gone—God knows I had given him every reason, and I wouldn't have been surprised if he had. And yet he stayed and helped me fight my way back.

And I know I have been equally blessed with my family, my friends, my children, my community. But what of the victims without these blessings?

What of those whose husbands and lovers do leave them, unable or unwilling to handle what comes after a rape? What about those in homeless shelters, hiding from batterers? What of those who will never get help and support, because they cannot, will not, tell this secret? And what of those victims who are men, our brothers, shamed into a pain no less than mine, but, if possible, even less acceptable?

I've spoken out for laws that I thought were good ones, and against laws that I thought were bad ones. But I wonder: If where we begin this battle is with tougher laws, longer sentences, and bigger prisons, aren't we starting too late? Sometimes I feel like shouting into the wind, "Somebody better hurry up and solve this mess right now! Because my sons and my daughter are already here!"

I don't pretend to know where rape comes from. I'm certainly no stranger to anger, but I can't begin to understand the kind of anger that gives way to sexual abuse. Over the past two or three years, I've read a lot of books and talked to a lot of people. All I have are facts; I don't know if I'll ever have understanding.

I know I am no longer who I was, not just because of what happened to me but because of everything that came after: the fight for recovery, the trial, the publicity. And I'm not sure yet just exactly who or what it is that I'm becoming—only time will tell me that.

However, I do know who I am not: Joan of Arc, or Mother Teresa, or Saint Nancy of the Rape Crisis Center. I don't have all the answers; I don't even have all the questions yet. But one of the most important things I've learned is that I found my sanity when I found my voice. I've learned that to *witness* is to speak out, to name the unnameable, to turn and face it down.

But I would never judge those victims who decide they must remain silent—they are my sisters, and my brothers, and this hard choice must be theirs alone. And when your attacker is your husband, or your favorite uncle, or your father, or your best friend, who could blame you if you "just want to forget it"?

If there is a message to my story, it is this: There are no fairy tales left in this world, and no magic wands to fix what's gone terribly wrong. There are damsels in distress, all right, but no more knights in shining armor to slay the damn dragons, and no high castle walls to hide behind. If there are solutions, they are not simple, and they are not easy.

But there's a strength inside each of us that we don't even know is there. To help us find it, there are people with good hearts and good brains, who do what they do every day, in spite of budgets that shrink and statistics that climb and communities that turn away from the truth.

I believe with all my heart that there can be no forgetting, and precious little chance of healing, until you decide to *tell someone*. There are so many levels of telling: a friend, a parent, a lover, a brother or sister, a minister, your doctor, a mental-health professional, a cop. Get help, from wherever you can, and ask for what you need until you get it. It is your absolute right, and it may be your only salvation.

One day I walked for hours on that beach in Virginia, looking out at the ocean, imagining all the beauty beneath it, beauty that somehow survives in spite of being a long way from the sun. It was calm that day, but I knew it wouldn't always be. Storms come. And when faced with the pain and terror and loneliness, you can easily give in, and drown.

Or, with all the rage and life force inside you, you can decide to fight to make it to shore. Given the choice—or, if not given it, then *taking* it—I say fight back. Fight like hell and head for the beach. The survivors are already there waiting for you. With chocolate.

AFTERWORD

My heartfelt thanks to:

- Mom, Crampa, and Gramma: for raising me with the strength and courage all of this took;
- Ronnie and Diane: for always standing by me no matter what;
- Penny: for making sure I didn't lose my mind when I thought I'd lost everything;
- Cathy Burnham: for telling me that I was not alone when I thought I was;
- Bill Olson: for allowing me to grow up in your office;
- Jeannie P.: for the endless grammatical corrections and for not bringing your law books when we traveled together;
- Carol: for your patience and your countless hours of typing and scheduling;
- Ralph Roth: for giving me reason to believe;
- Dee Ann Wolfe: for listening, for holding my hand;
- Cindy Arbelbide: for the hours you spent finding information, and for helping me understand it;
- Nan Horvat: for making the system work, and for taking the time to let me yell;
- Roger Owens and Cindy Moisan: for the defense, and for teaching me what that meant;
- Geneva Overholser: for the invitation to tell the story;
- Jane Schorer: for all the months of work, and all the tears;
- All the friends who listened, but never judged;

- LARKIN W.: for being my co-author, but most of all for being my friend;
- Every rape victim: for your courage, which every single day helps me find my own.

- STEVEN and the children: for everything, for always.

RESOURCES

Center for the Study and
Prevention of Campus
Violence
Room 305, Administration
Building
Towson State University
Towson, MD 21204
(301) 830-2178

Crime Victims Research &
Treatment Center
Medical University of South
Carolina
171 Ashley Avenue
Charleston, SC 29425
(803) 792-2945

Criminal Justice Statistics
Association
444 North Capitol Street NW,
Suite 606
Washington, DC 20001
(202) 624-8560

Defensive Living
2539 West Royal Lane, Suite
1711

Irving, TX 75063
(214) 402-9537

Iowa Coalition Against Sexual
Abuse
Illinois Hall
25th and Carpenter
Des Moines, IA 50311
(515) 242-5096

National Association of Crime
Victim Compensation Boards
1900 L Street NW, Suite 500
Washington, DC 20036
(202) 293-5420

National Center for
Post-traumatic Stress
Disorder
Veterans Administration
Medical and Regional Office
Center 116D
White River Junction, VT
05009
(802) 296-5132

National Coalition Against
Sexual Abuse (NCASA)
2722 Eastlake Avenue East,
Suite 220
Seattle, WA 98102
(206) 328-8588

National Crime Prevention
Council
1700 K Street NW
Washington, DC 20006
(202) 466-6272

National Crime Prevention
Institute
School of Justice
Administration
College of Urban and Public
Affairs
Louisville, KY 40292
(502) 588-6987

National Organization for
Victim Assistance (NOVA)
1757 Park Road NW
Washington, DC 20010
(202) 232-6682

National Organization for
Women
1000 16th Street NW, Suite
700
Washington, DC 20036
(202) 331-0066

National Woman Abuse
Prevention Project
2000 P Street NW, Suite 508
Washington, DC 20036
(202) 857-0216

Santa Monica Rape Treatment
Crisis Center
Santa Monica Hospital Medical
Center
1250 16th Street
Santa Monica, CA 90404
(213) 319-4000

Violence and Victims
(publication)
Springer Publishing Company
536 Broadway
New York, NY 10012
(212) 431-4370

Newsletters, brochures, and other publications can be obtained from most of these organizations for little or no cost. Additional information can be found in the white or yellow pages of your local telephone book, or through your local or county rape crisis center or victim's assistance/resource center.